D1190976

COLLECTED POEMS
OF HENRY THOREAU

COLLECTED POEMS
of
Henry Thoreau

 m

edited by
Carl Bode

PACKARD AND COMPANY
CHICAGO, 1943

McCORMICK THEOLOGICAL
SEMINARY LIBRARY,
CHICAGO

COPYRIGHT, 1943, BY PACKARD AND COMPANY

All rights reserved

First Trade Edition

DESIGNED BY BERT KEMPSHALL, CHICAGO, AND
PRINTED IN THE UNITED STATES OF AMERICA
BY PANTAGRAPH PRESS, BLOOMINGTON, ILLINOIS

PS
3041
B 666

8707

To
MY FRIENDS IN
THE THOREAU SOCIETY

INTRODUCTION

"The purest strain, and the loftiest, I think, that has yet pealed from this unpoetic American forest," Ralph Waldo Emerson declared after being shown an early poem of Thoreau's.

A week later he wrote across the ocean to Thomas Carlyle about this young poet named Thoreau, who was writing "the truest verses." To the surprise of Concord, Emerson proceeded to act as evangelist for the poetry of his shy and prickly neighbor. But by 1841, two years after the letter to Carlyle, his enthusiasm had begun to cool. At that time the *Dial* was already being published, with Emerson and Margaret Fuller in charge of selecting the material to go into it. There the evangelist yielded to the editor; and Thoreau's verse, far from sacred, was exposed to heavy editorial suggestion or to rejection. And then, a year or so later, we know that Thoreau destroyed many of the verses he had written—destroyed them at the instance of Emerson, "who did not praise them."

There, in forecast, is the history of Thoreau's reputation as a poet. A hundred years ago, great men—as they are now reckoned in American literature—talked about his poems. Not always esteemed, the verses were by no means ignored. Bronson Alcott applauded them; Lowell asserted their rawness; Hawthorne gave them a grudging approval. Yet by about 1847 Thoreau's prose was beginning its bid for recognition; and soon, in his own eyes and in the eyes of his circle, Thoreau began to be viewed as a writer whose destined medium was prose. By the time of his death he was known to the discerning as a man to be reckoned with in American letters. By the turn of the century, Thoreau, author of *Walden*, was world-renowned. And Thoreau the poet was forgotten.

The world thus repeated Emerson's change of attitude toward Thoreau's verse. But there was a difference. Emerson afterward achieved a balanced judgment. His early praise and his later criticism corrected one another, and his final verdict, prepared shortly after Thoreau died, gave the poetry measured praise. In Thoreau's work, pronounced Emerson, it was true that the gold did "not yet run pure," was "drossy and crude." But still, it was gold. Then too, although Thoreau lacked technical ease, he had the genius of the true poet. Moreover, Emerson added, in a comment that was often to be echoed, Thoreau's "biography is in his verses."

That the poetry Henry Thoreau scrawled and labored over, and later neglected, has its defects as well as its values, no one would deny. Yet almost every bit of the verse has a dry, oblique power. It has, moreover, the virtue of lighting up its creator's life. There is of course the biography of the heart and the biography of the mind. The poems can help us to understand both. On the one hand, for example, Thoreau's earnest love for Ellen Sewall is illuminated in the lyrics he wrote when she came into his life. On the other, his rigid principle of intellect is revealed in such a poem as "Wait not till slaves pronounce the word," where his searching advice to the abolitionists is to remember that there are more forms of slavery besides negro slavery, there are subtler masters enchaining us all.

A generation before Emerson's penetrating remark, Thoreau himself had spoken to the point, saying "Poetry is a piece of very private history, which unostentatiously lets us into the secret of a man's life." Indeed, though Thoreau came to see, as everyone still does, that prose was his medium, he by no means overlooked the importance of poetry. For several years after graduation from "Cambridge College" he considered himself a practicing poet. Much of the large amount of verse he mentions writing has not come down to us, but what is left still forms a far larger body than a glance through his collected works might lead anyone to think. Furthermore, Thoreau did not confine himself to the actual production of poems. He found time to develop and set forth a considerable poetics. His statements about poetry and the poet are scattered through both the books and essays, and the Journal. In synthesis they embody a theory that is shrewd as well as intuitive. Thoreau, as a matter of record, maintained his interest in the theory of poetry long after he abandoned the practice. Jottings about the function of the poet appear in the Journal almost to the end. True, by then Thoreau had widened the definition of his important terms, *poet* and *poetry*, but his final comments still showed no basic conflict with his earliest pronouncements. So Thoreau theorized for nearly three decades but composed poems, with zeal, for only a handful of years. In that fact lies one of the main causes for the long-continued neglect of his verse by others. Thoreau's own loss of interest was duplicated by that of the rest of the world.

There are, on analysis, three major reasons why most persons have ignored Thoreau's poetry. The first in importance, perhaps, is its uneven quality. The second, and related, reason is the fact that he himself lost enthusiasm for the poetic medium; the quantity of his production quickly dwindled. The third is the mistaken belief that the verses are mere fragments woven into the prose, especially in the *Week*, and inseparable from it.

The quality and quantity of Thoreau's verse marched side by side during his literary career. When he wrote the most poetry, he was writing the best poetry—with one nearly inevitable qualification. Thoreau did improve, for a while, in his craft as he practiced it. He first paid distinct attention to verse writing in his final college years. His attempts at that time and up to about 1839 were uneven and mainly derivative. Among the best were "I am a parcel of vain strivings tied" and the 1838 "Friendship"; the worst included such an effusion as "My Boots." Soon he began to find his own style and approach, and, with a lapse in 1840, the years from 1839 through 1842 were his most skillful and productive. The readers of that radical publication, the *Dial*, were privileged to see some of the finest—in part despite editorial pressure and in part perhaps because of it—among Thoreau's poems. But the *Dial* did not live long, and by the time of its demise the output and quality of Thoreau's poetry had sagged. The most remarkable poems that he inserted in the 1849 *Week* were the very ones he had published in the *Dial* seven and eight years earlier. By February, 1852, Thoreau noted dryly but sadly:

> The strains from my muse are as rare nowadays,
> or of late years, as the notes of birds in the winter,—
> the faintest occasional tinkling sound, and mostly of

the woodpecker kind or the harsh jay or crow. It never melts into a song.

The verse used in *Walden*, except for the reprinted "Light-winged Smoke, Icarian bird," was negligible. The last few pieces set down in the Journal, aside from one final lyric of 1857, slid into prose. Then, aside from a line or so, Thoreau was done.

The third reason for the general neglect of his verse was given its fullest expression in the preface to the little volume of Thoreau's poetry, *Poems of Nature*, published in 1895. Explaining that it included only two-thirds (actually much less) of the available material, the editors, H. S. Salt and F. B. Sanborn, apologized for not printing more. Many lyrics, they argued, were nothing but pendants to Thoreau's prose; were little bits of verse, so interwoven that it would have been unjust, artistically, to wrench them from their context. The editors had the prose of the *Week* particularly in mind. It does have a great deal of verse apparently imbedded in it. Because the view put forth by Salt and Sanborn must be faced by anyone compiling a fuller edition of the poems, it ought at this point briefly to be examined. Was their stand well taken?

A study of the *Week* will tell. Close to a dozen of the fullest and most important poems in it had already been published, as separate poems, elsewhere. Most of them had appeared in the *Dial*, and all Thoreau did when he put them into the *Week* was to cut off their titles. In three cases he did not even do that. Besides these poems, there was a considerable number of others which Thoreau had composed, again separately, in his Journal. Later these were polished and inserted in the *Week*. A third group consists of fragments. They, it is true, are hard to separate from their prose context. On the other hand, these fragments are often parts of longer poems Thoreau had written, and can be collated against the full versions from which he took them. For example, Thoreau used half a dozen snatches of "The Assabet" and "Inspiration" in the *Week*. Yet they all exist as parts of these long full poems. There are also a few poems which are actually so interwoven in the prose that they contain references to the prose surrounding them. In those cases, a synopsis of the context has been added in the notes to the Critical Edition. There remain, finally, three or four poems that are fragmentary not through any fault of Thoreau's but because their opening pages have been cut out of the Journal in which he wrote them. To sum up, the great number of his poems can stand as entities and by themselves.

Here, then, is every available piece of original verse that Henry Thoreau composed. With only about half a dozen exceptions, it has the authority either of publication during his own life or else of his own autograph. In general, the posthumous verse is for the first time presented exactly—allowing for editorial error—as he wrote it. The glowing lines and the quiet, the prosaic and the Transcendental—they are all here. Almost all have at the very least the large, astringent force of young genius. Thoreau himself, let it be said, was pleased when his poetry won someone's commendation; but all, surely, that Thoreau would have needed to ask of the reader then or now, a century ago or today, is what his admired Wordsworth asked:

> One request I must make of my Reader, which is, that in judging these Poems, he would decide by his own feelings genuinely.

ACKNOWLEDGMENTS

For permission to use manuscripts of Thoreau's verse I am indebted to the Abernethy Library of American Literature, Middlebury College; the Harvard College Library; the Henry E. Huntington Library and Art Gallery; Mr. Albert Edgar Lownes; the Pierpont Morgan Library; the New York Public Library; Mr. W. Stephen Thomas; and the Yale University Library. The Houghton Mifflin Company has allowed me to quote from material by Thoreau, in particular, the published Journal and *Poems of Nature*, for which it holds the copyright.

I wish also to acknowledge the helpfulness of Professors Elsie F. Brickett and Gay W. Allen, who lent photostats and microfilms respectively. Dr. Viola White, besides preparing typescripts of the verse in the Abernethy Library, answered numerous questions connected with the edition; Miss Edythe N. Backus was responsible for the important Huntington Library transcriptions; and Mr. John Colwell recollated the poetry in the Harvard College Library. The painstaking secretarial help of Mrs. John W. Rau, Jr. and of Miss Dorothy Garrett has been invaluable. Nor should I want to take for granted the thorough coöperation afforded me by the librarians of Northwestern University and Keuka College. Henry Seidel Canby's careful and comprehensive biography has, for our generation, made any additional life of Thoreau unnecessary; and I have often drawn on his book for my notes, in the Critical

Edition of the *Collected Poems,* on the content of the verse. Both Dr. Canby and Dr. Arthur Christy furthered the progress of my edition with information at their disposal; Mr. Walter Harding, secretary of the Thoreau Society, kindly checked the references about the Thoreau country in the notes to the Critical Edition; and Professor Walter Hendricks was responsible for directing the book through the press.

This edition was first suggested to me by Professor Leon Howard of Northwestern University, and it owes much to his learning and common sense. My debt, finally, to my wife is great—how great, only someone who has undertaken a project like mine could appreciate.

January 4, 1943   C. B.
Keuka Park, New York

CONTENTS

* Titles of the poems are those drawn from the basic texts. If Thoreau omitted the title from the final version of a poem, the first line is used here, even though he may have given a title to earlier versions. Earlier titles, however, as well as those assigned by prior editors, are placed immediately below the title given. See also the Index of Titles and First Lines.

COLLECTED POEMS
OF HENRY THOREAU

NOTE ON THE ORDER OF THE POEMS

Of the poems published mainly while Thoreau was still living those on pages 3-22 made their final appearance, during his lifetime, in the *Dial* and other periodicals. The only posthumously printed verses in this section, aside from "Carpe Diem," appeared in articles for which Thoreau had at least partly corrected the proofs and which came out in the *Atlantic Monthly* shortly after his death. The periodical verse is arranged in the order of publication; the couplets, however, are grouped together at the end of this section as are the couplets in succeeding sections. The quatrain on page 23 Thoreau printed in the 1849 edition of *A Week on the Concord and Merrimack Rivers* but dropped from the revised edition. The poems on pages 24-27 are the ones to be found in *Walden*, and the quatrain on page 28 first appeared in the 1864 edition of *The Maine Woods*. The poetry on pages 29-85 comes from the 1868 edition of the *Week*. When Thoreau revised the *Week* for this second edition, it should be noted, he made very few changes in the text of the poems; and he added only one quatrain and a couplet.

Of the poems unpublished during Thoreau's lifetime those on pages 86-187 have a date of composition determined, with the final date, if there are two or more, dictating where the poem is placed. The verse in this section is arranged chronologically. The poems without a known date of composition are divided into those having manuscript authority and those lacking it. Verse with manuscript authority, pages 188-229, is drawn from the noted Thoreau collections and is grouped according to those sources. This order is less arbitrary than it may first seem, since each major manuscript holding happens to have some homogeneity. The order of the poems within each manuscript holding, aside from that of the Huntington Library, is determined by a variety of external and internal factors. The succession of the Huntington Library poems is based on the Library's own tentative chronology. Verse without manuscript authority either entirely or for the basic text here in the *Collected Poems* is arranged according to the order of publication of its printed sources, and is to be found on pages 230-243. Finally, poems of doubtful authenticity, as well as miscellanea, are given on pages 244-247.

Within the circuit of this plodding life
There enter moments of an azure hue,
Untarnished fair as is the violet
Or anemone, when the spring strews them
By some meandering rivulet, which make
The best philosophy untrue that aims
But to console man for his grievances.
I have remembered when the winter came,
High in my chamber in the frosty nights,
When in the still light of the cheerful moon,
On every twig and rail and jutting spout,
The icy spears were adding to their length
Against the arrows of the coming sun,
How in the shimmering noon of summer past
Some unrecorded beam slanted across
The upland pastures where the Johnswort grew;
Or heard, amid the verdure of my mind,
The bee's long smothered hum, on the blue flag
Loitering amidst the mead; or busy rill,
Which now through all its course stands still and dumb
Its own memorial,—purling at its play
Along the slopes, and through the meadows next,
Until its youthful sound was hushed at last
In the staid current of the lowland stream;
Or seen the furrows shine but late upturned,
And where the fieldfare followed in the rear,
When all the fields around lay bound and hoar
Beneath a thick integument of snow.
So by God's cheap economy made rich
To go upon my winter's task again.

His steady sails he never furls
At any time o' year,
And perching now on Winter's curls,
He whistles in his ear.

Sometimes I hear the veery's clarion,
Or brazen trump of the impatient jay,
And in secluded woods the chicadee
Doles out her scanty notes, which sing the praise
Of heroes, and set forth the loveliness
Of virtue evermore.

Upon the lofty elm tree sprays
The vireo rings the changes sweet,
During the trivial summer days,
Striving to lift our thoughts above the street.

Thou dusky spirit of the wood,
Bird of an ancient brood,
Flitting thy lonely way,
A meteor in the summer's day,
From wood to wood, from hill to hill,
Low over forest, field and rill,
What wouldst thou say?
Why shouldst thou haunt the day?
What makes thy melancholy float?
What bravery inspires thy throat,
And bears thee up above the clouds,
Over desponding human crowds,
Which far below
Lay thy haunts low?

The river swelleth more and more,
Like some sweet influence stealing o'er
The passive town; and for a while
Each tussuck makes a tiny isle,
Where, on some friendly Ararat,
Resteth the weary water-rat.

No ripple shows Musketaquid,
Her very current e'en is hid,
As deepest souls do calmest rest,
When thoughts are swelling in the breast,
And she that in the summer's drought
Doth make a rippling and a rout,
Sleeps from Nahshawtuck to the Cliff,
Unruffled by a single skiff.
But by a thousand distant hills
The louder roar a thousand rills,
And many a spring which now is dumb,
And many a stream with smothered hum,
Doth swifter well and faster glide,
Though buried deep beneath the tide.

Our village shows a rural Venice,
Its broad lagoons where yonder fen is;
As lovely as the Bay of Naples
Yon placid cove amid the maples;
And in my neighbor's field of corn
I recognise the Golden Horn.

Here Nature taught from year to year,
When only red men came to hear,
Methinks 'twas in this school of art
Venice and Naples learned their part,
But still their mistress, to my mind,
Her young disciples leaves behind.

Great God, I ask thee for no meaner pelf
Than that I may not disappoint myself,
That in my action I may soar as high,
As I can now discern with this clear eye.

And next in value, which thy kindness lends,
That I may greatly disappoint my friends,
Howe'er they think or hope that it may be,
They may not dream how thou'st distinguished me.

That my weak hand may equal my firm faith,
And my life practice more than my tongue saith;
That my low conduct may not show,
Nor my relenting lines,
That I thy purpose did not know,
Or overrated thy designs.

THE MOON

Time wears her not; she doth his chariot guide;
Mortality below her orb is placed.
—*Raleigh.*

The full-orbed moon with unchanged ray
  Mounts up the eastern sky,
Not doomed to these short nights for aye,
  But shining steadily.

She does not wane, but my fortune,
  Which her rays do not bless,
My wayward path declineth soon,
  But she shines not the less.

And if she faintly glimmers here,
  And paled is her light,
Yet alway in her proper sphere
  She's mistress of the night.

TO A STRAY FOWL

Poor bird! destined to lead thy life
    Far in the adventurous west,
And here to be debarred to-night
    From thy accustomed nest;
Must thou fall back upon old instinct now—
Well nigh extinct under man's fickle care?
Did heaven bestow its quenchless inner light
So long ago, for thy small want to-night?
Why stand'st upon thy toes to crow so late?
The moon is deaf to thy low feathered fate;
Or dost thou think so to possess the night,
And people the drear dark with thy brave sprite?
And now with anxious eye thou look'st about,
While the relentless shade draws on its veil,
For some sure shelter from approaching dews,
And the insidious steps of nightly foes.
I fear imprisonment has dulled thy wit,
Or ingrained servitude extinguished it.
But no—dim memory of the days of yore,
By Brahmapootra and the Jumna's shore,
Where thy proud race flew swiftly o'er the heath,
And sought its food the jungle's shade beneath,
Has taught thy wings to seek yon friendly trees,
As erst by Indus' banks and far Ganges.

THE SLUGGISH SMOKE CURLS UP
FROM SOME DEEP DELL

The sluggish smoke curls up from some deep dell,
The stiffened air exploring in the dawn,
And making slow acquaintance with the day;
Delaying now upon its heavenward course,
In wreathed loiterings dallying with itself,
With as uncertain purpose and slow deed,
As its half-wakened master by the hearth,
Whose mind still slumbering and sluggish thoughts
Have not yet swept into the onward current
Of the new day;—and now it streams afar,
The while the chopper goes with step direct,
And mind intent to swing the early axe.
  First in the dusky dawn he sends abroad
His early scout, his emissary, smoke,
The earliest, latest pilgrim from the roof,
To feel the frosty air, inform the day;
And while he crouches still beside the hearth,
Nor musters courage to unbar the door,
It has gone down the glen with the light wind,
And o'er the plain unfurled its venturous wreath,
Draped the tree tops, loitered upon the hill,
And warmed the pinions of the early bird;
And now, perchance, high in the crispy air,
Has caught sight of the day o'er the earth's edge,
And greets its master's eye at his low door,
As some refulgent cloud in the upper sky.

When Winter fringes every bough
  With his fantastic wreath,
And puts the seal of silence now
  Upon the leaves beneath;

When every stream in its pent-house
  Goes gurgling on its way,
And in his gallery the mouse
  Nibbleth the meadow hay;

Methinks the summer still is nigh,
  And lurketh underneath,
As that same meadow mouse doth lie
  Snug in the last year's heath.

And if perchance the chicadee
  Lisp a faint note anon,
The snow in summer's canopy,
  Which she herself put on.

Fair blossoms deck the cheerful trees,
  And dazzling fruits depend,
The north wind sighs a summer breeze,
  The nipping frosts to fend,

Bringing glad tidings unto me,
  The while I stand all ear,
Of a serene eternity,
  Which need not winter fear.

Out on the silent pond straightway
  The restless ice doth crack,
And pond sprites merry gambols play
  Amid the deafening rack.

Eager I hasten to the vale,
  As if I heard brave news,
How nature held high festival,
  Which it were hard to lose.

I gambol with my neighbor ice,
  And sympathizing quake,
As each new crack darts in a trice
  Across the gladsome lake.

One with the cricket in the ground,
  And faggot on the hearth,
Resounds the rare domestic sound
  Along the forest path.

NOT UNCONCERNED WACHUSETT
REARS HIS HEAD

Not unconcerned Wachusett rears his head
  Above the field, so late from nature won,
With patient brow reserved, as one who read
  New annals in the history of man.

Where they once dug for money,
But never found any;
Where sometimes Martial Miles
Singly files,
And Elijah Wood,
I fear for no good:
No other man,
Save Elisha Dugan,—
O man of wild habits,
Partridges and rabbits,
Who hast no cares
Only to set snares,
Who liv'st all alone,
Close to the bone,
And where life is sweetest
Constantly eatest.
When the spring stirs my blood
With the instinct to travel,
I can get enough gravel
On the Old Marlborough Road.
Nobody repairs it,
For nobody wears it;
It is a living way,
As the Christians say.
Not many there be
Who enter therein,
Only the guests of the
Irishman Quin.

What is it, what is it,
  But a direction out there,
And the bare possibility
  Of going somewhere?
      Great guide-boards of stone,
      But travellers none;
      Cenotaphs of the towns
      Named on their crowns.
      It is worth going to see
      Where you *might* be.
      What king
      Did the thing,
      I am still wondering;
      Set up how or when,
      By what selectmen,
      Gourgas or Lee,
      Clark or Darby?
      They're a great endeavor
      To be something forever;
      Blank tablets of stone,
      Where a traveller might groan,
      And in one sentence
      Grave all that it known;
      Which another might read,
      In his extreme need.
      I know one or two
      Lines that would do,
      Literature that might stand
      All over the land,
      Which a man could remember
      Till next December,

And read again in the spring,
  After the thawing.
If with fancy unfurled
  You leave your abode,
You may go round the world
  By the Old Marlborough Road.

In two years' time 't had thus
   Reached the level of the rocks,
Admired the stretching world,
   Nor feared the wandering flocks.

But at this tender age
   Its sufferings began:
There came a browsing ox
   And cut it down a span.

CARPE DIEM

Build not on to-morrow,
　But seize on to-day!
From no future borrow,
　The present to pay.

Wait not any longer
　Thy work to begin;
The worker grows stronger,—
　Be steadfast and win!

Forbode not new sorrow—
　Bear that of to-day,
And trust that the morrow
　Shall chase it away.

The task of the present
　Be sure to fulfil;
If sad, or if pleasant,
　Be true to it still.

God sendeth us sorrow
　And cloudeth our day;
His sun on the morrow
　Shines bright on our way.

EACH SUMMER SOUND

Each summer sound
Is a summer round.

THE NEEDLES OF THE PINE

The needles of the pine,
All to the west incline.

IN THE EAST FAMES ARE WON

In the East fames are won,
In the West deeds are done.

LOVE EQUALS SWIFT AND SLOW

Love equals swift and slow,
   And high and low,
Racer and lame,
   The hunter and his game.

MEN SAY THEY KNOW
MANY THINGS

Men say they know many things;
But lo! they have taken wings,—
The arts and sciences,
And a thousand appliances;
The wind that blows
Is all that any body knows.

WHAT'S THE RAILROAD TO ME

What's the railroad to me?
I never go to see
Where it ends.
It fills a few hollows,
And makes banks for the swallows,
It sets the sand a-blowing,
And the blackberries a-growing,

It is no dream of mine,
To ornament a line;
I cannot come nearer to God and Heaven
Than I live to Walden even.
I am its stony shore,
And the breeze that passes o'er;
In the hollow of my hand
Are its water and its sand,
And its deepest resort
Lies high in my thought.

LIGHT-WINGED SMOKE, ICARIAN BIRD

Light-winged Smoke, Icarian bird,
Melting thy pinions in thy upward flight,
Lark without song, and messenger of dawn,
Circling above the hamlets as thy nest;
Or else, departing dream, and shadowy form
Of midnight vision, gathering up thy skirts;
By night star-veiling, and by day
Darkening the light and blotting out the sun;
Go thou my incense upward from this hearth,
And ask the gods to pardon this clear flame.

Die and be buried who will,
   I mean to live here still;
My nature grows ever more young
   The primitive pines among.

WHERE'ER THOU SAIL'ST
WHO SAILED WITH ME

Where'er thou sail'st who sailed with me,
Though now thou climbest loftier mounts,
And fairer rivers dost ascend,
Be thou my Muse, my Brother—.

I AM BOUND, I AM BOUND, FOR A DISTANT SHORE

I am bound, I am bound, for a distant shore,
By a lonely isle, by a far Azore,
There it is, there it is, the treasure I seek,
On the barren sands of a desolate creek.

I SAILED UP A RIVER WITH A PLEASANT WIND

I sailed up a river with a pleasant wind,
New lands, new people, and new thoughts to find;
Many fair reaches and headlands appeared,
And many dangers were there to be feared;
But when I remember where I have been,
And the fair landscapes that I have seen,
THOU seemest the only permanent shore,
The cape never rounded, nor wandered o'er.

The respectable folks,—
Where dwell they?
They whisper in the oaks,
And they sigh in the hay;
Summer and winter, night and day,
Out on the meadow, there dwell they.
They never die,
Nor snivel, nor cry,
Nor ask our pity
With a wet eye.
A sound estate they ever mend,
To every asker readily lend;
To the ocean wealth,
To the meadow health,
To Time his length,
To the rocks strength,
To the stars light,
To the weary night,
To the busy day,
To the idle play;
And so their good cheer never ends,
For all are their debtors, and all their friends.

Ah, 'tis in vain the peaceful din
   That wakes the ignoble town,
Not thus did braver spirits win
   A patriot's renown.

There is one field beside this stream,
   Wherein no foot does fall,
But yet it beareth in my dream
   A richer crop than all.

Let me believe a dream so dear,
   Some heart beat high that day,
Above the petty Province here,
   And Britain far away;

Some hero of the ancient mould,
   Some arm of knightly worth,
Of strength unbought, and faith unsold,
   Honored this spot of earth;

Who sought the prize his heart described,
   And did not ask release,
Whose free-born valor was not bribed
   By prospect of a peace.

The men who stood on yonder height
   That day are long since gone;
Not the same hand directs the fight
   And monumental stone.

Ye were the Grecian cities then,
  The Romes of modern birth,
Where the New England husbandmen
  Have shown a Roman worth.

In vain I search a foreign land
  To find our Bunker Hill,
And Lexington and Concord stand
  By no Laconian rill.

But since we sailed
Some things have failed,
And many a dream
Gone down the stream.

Here then an aged shepherd dwelt,
Who to his flock his substance dealt,
And ruled them with a vigorous crook,
By precept of the sacred Book;
But he the pierless bridge passed o'er,
And solitary left the shore.

Anon a youthful pastor came,
Whose crook was not unknown to fame,
His lambs he viewed with gentle glance,
Spread o'er the country's wide expanse,
And fed with "Mosses from the Manse."
Here was our Hawthorne in the dale,
And here the shepherd told his tale.

On Ponkawtasset, since, we took our way,
Down this still stream to far Billericay,
A poet wise has settled, whose fine ray
Doth often shine on Concord's twilight day.

Like those first stars, whose silver beams on high,
Shining more brightly as the day goes by,
Most travellers cannot at first descry,
But eyes that wont to range the evening sky,

And know celestial lights, do plainly see,
And gladly hail them, numbering two or three;
For lore that's deep must deeply studied be,
As from deep wells men read star-poetry.

These stars are never paled, though out of sight,
But like the sun they shine forever bright;
Ay, *they* are suns, though earth must in its flight
Put out its eyes that it may see their light.

Who would neglect the least celestial sound,
Or faintest light that falls on earthly ground,
If he could know it one day would be found
That star in Cygnus whither we are bound,
And pale our sun with heavenly radiance round?

AN EARLY UNCONVERTED SAINT

An early unconverted Saint,
Free from noontide or evening taint,
Heathen without reproach,
That did upon the civil day encroach,
And ever since its birth
Had trod the outskirts of the earth.

Low in the eastern sky
Is set thy glancing eye;
And though its gracious light
Ne'er riseth to my sight,
Yet every star that climbs
Above the gnarled limbs
    Of yonder hill,
Conveys thy gentle will.

Believe I knew thy thought,
And that the zephyrs brought
Thy kindest wishes through,
As mine they bear to you,
That some attentive cloud
Did pause amid the crowd
    Over my head,
While gentle things were said.

Believe the thrushes sung,
And that the flower-bells rung,
That herbs exhaled their scent,
And beasts knew what was meant,
The trees a welcome waved,
And lakes their margins laved,
    When thy free mind
To my retreat did wind.

It was a summer eve,
The air did gently heave
While yet a low-hung cloud
Thy eastern skies did shroud;
The lightning's silent gleam,
Startling my drowsy dream,
   Seemed like the flash
Under thy dark eyelash.

Still will I strive to be
As if thou wert with me;
Whatever path I take,
It shall be for thy sake,
Of gentle slope and wide,
As thou wert by my side,
   Without a root
To trip thy gentle foot.

I'll walk with gentle pace,
And choose the smoothest place,
And careful dip the oar,
And shun the winding shore,
And gently steer my boat
Where water-lilies float,
   And cardinal flowers
Stand in their sylvan bowers.

DONG, SOUNDS THE BRASS IN THE EAST

Dong, sounds the brass in the east,
As if to a funeral feast,
But I like that sound the best
Out of the fluttering west.

The steeple ringeth a knell,
But the fairies' silvery bell
Is the voice of that gentle folk,
Or else the horizon that spoke.

Its metal is not of brass,
But air, and water, and glass,
And under a cloud it is swung,
And by the wind it is rung.

When the steeple tolleth the noon,
It soundeth not so soon,
Yet it rings a far earlier hour,
And the sun has not reached its tower.

I make ye an offer,
Ye gods, hear the scoffer,
The scheme will not hurt you,
If ye will find goodness, I will find virtue.
Though I am your creature,
And child of your nature,
I have pride still unbended,
And blood undescended,
Some free independence,
And my own descendants.
I cannot toil blindly,
Though ye behave kindly,
And I swear by the rood,
I'll be slave to no God.
If ye will deal plainly,
I will strive mainly,
If ye will discover,
Great plans to your lover,
And give him a sphere
Somewhat larger than here.

Conscience is instinct bred in the house,
Feeling and Thinking propagate the sin
By an unnatural breeding in and in.
I say, Turn it out doors,
Into the moors.
I love a life whose plot is simple,
And does not thicken with every pimple,
A soul so sound no sickly conscience binds it,
That makes the universe no worse than 't finds it.
I love an earnest soul,
Whose mighty joy and sorrow
Are not drowned in a bowl,
And brought to life to-morrow;
That lives one tragedy,
And not seventy;
A conscience worth keeping,
Laughing not weeping;
A conscience wise and steady,
And forever ready;
Not changing with events,
Dealing in compliments;
A conscience exercised about
Large things, where one *may* doubt.
I love a soul not all of wood,
Predestinated to be good,
But true to the backbone
Unto itself alone,
And false to none;

Born to its own affairs,
Its own joys and own cares;
By whom the work which God begun
Is finished, and not undone;
Taken up where he left off,
Whether to worship or to scoff;
If not good, why then evil,
If not good god, good devil.
Goodness! you hypocrite, come out of that,
Live your life, do your work, then take your hat.
I have no patience towards
Such conscientious cowards.
Give me simple laboring folk,
Who love their work,
Whose virtue is a song
To cheer God along.

Such water do the gods distil,
And pour down every hill
   For their New England men;
A draught of this wild nectar bring,
And I'll not taste the spring
   Of Helicon again.

That Phaeton of our day,
Who'd make another milky way,
And burn the world up with his ray;

By us an undisputed seer,—
Who'd drive his flaming car so near
Unto our shuddering mortal sphere,

Disgracing all our slender worth,
And scorching up the living earth,
To prove his heavenly birth.

The silver spokes, the golden tire,
Are glowing with unwonted fire,
And ever nigher roll and nigher;

The pins and axle melted are,
The silver radii fly afar,
Ah, he will spoil his Father's car!

Who let him have the steeds he cannot steer?
Henceforth the sun will not shine for a year;
And we shall Ethiops all appear.

Though all the fates should prove unkind,
Leave not your native land behind.
The ship, becalmed, at length stands still;
The steed must rest beneath the hill;
But swiftly still our fortunes pace
To find us out in every place.

The vessel, though her masts be firm,
Beneath her copper bears a worm;
Around the cape, across the line,
Till fields of ice her course confine;
It matters not how smooth the breeze,
How shallow or how deep the seas,
Whether she bears Manilla twine,
Or in her hold Madeira wine,
Or China teas, or Spanish hides,
In port or quarantine she rides;
Far from New England's blustering shore,
New England's worm her hulk shall bore,
And sink her in the Indian seas,
Twine, wine, and hides, and China teas.

WITH FRONTIER STRENGTH YE STAND YOUR GROUND

With frontier strength ye stand your ground,
With grand content ye circle round,
Tumultuous silence for all sound,
Ye distant nursery of rills,
Monadnock and the Peterborough Hills;—
Firm argument that never stirs,
Outcircling the philosophers,—
Like some vast fleet,
Sailing through rain and sleet,
Through winter's cold and summer's heat;
Still holding on upon your high emprise,
Until ye find a shore amid the skies;
Not skulking close to land,
With cargo contraband,
For they who sent a venture out by ye
Have set the Sun to see
Their honesty.
Ships of the line, each one,
Ye westward run,
Convoying clouds,
Which cluster in your shrouds,
Always before the gale,
Under a press of sail,
With weight of metal all untold,—
I seem to feel ye in my firm seat here,
Immeasurable depth of hold,
And breadth of beam, and length of running gear.

Methinks ye take luxurious pleasure
In your novel western leisure;
So cool your brows and freshly blue,
As Time had naught for ye to do;
For ye lie at your length,
An unappropriated strength,
Unhewn primeval timber,
For knees so stiff, for masts so limber;
The stock of which new earths are made,
One day to be our *western* trade,
Fit for the stanchions of a world
Which through the seas of space is hurled.

While we enjoy a lingering ray,
Ye still o'ertop the western day,
Reposing yonder on God's croft
Like solid stacks of hay;
So bold a line as ne'er was writ
On any page by human wit;
The forest glows as if
An enemy's camp-fires shone
Along the horizon,
Or the day's funeral pyre
Were lighted there;
Edged with silver and with gold,
The clouds hang o'er in damask fold,
And with such depth of amber light
The west is dight,
Where still a few rays slant,
That even Heaven seems extravagant.

Watatic Hill
Lies on the horizon's sill
Like a child's toy left overnight,
And other duds to left and right,
On the earth's edge, mountains and trees
Stand as they were on air graven,
Or as the vessels in a haven
Await the morning breeze.
I fancy even
Through your defiles windeth the way to heaven;
And yonder still, in spite of history's page,
Linger the golden and the silver age;
Upon the laboring gale
The news of future centuries is brought,
And of new dynasties of thought,
From your remotest vale.

But special I remember thee,
Wachusett, who like me
Standest alone without society.
Thy far blue eye,
A remnant of the sky,
Seen through the clearing or the gorge,
Or from the windows of the forge,
Doth leaven all it passes by.
Nothing is true
But stands 'tween me and you,
Thou western pioneer,
Who know'st not shame nor fear,
By venturous spirit driven
Under the eaves of heaven;

And canst expand thee there,
And breathe enough of air?
Even beyond the West
Thou migratest,
Into unclouded tracts,
Without a pilgrim's axe,
Cleaving thy road on high
With thy well-tempered brow,
And mak'st thyself a clearing in the sky.
Upholding heaven, holding down earth,
Thy pastime from thy birth;
Not steadied by the one, nor leaning on the other,
May I approve myself thy worthy brother!

HERE LIES AN
HONEST MAN

Here lies an honest man,
Rear-Admiral Van.

———

Faith, then ye have
Two in one grave,
For in his favor,
Here too lies the Engraver.

The western wind came lumbering in,
Bearing a faint Pacific din,
Our evening mail, swift at the call
Of its Postmaster General;
Laden with news from Californ',
Whate'er transpired hath since morn,
How wags the world by brier and brake
From hence to Athabasca Lake;—

There is a vale which none hath seen,
Where foot of man has never been,
Such as here lives with toil and strife,
An anxious and a sinful life.

There every virtue has its birth,
Ere it descends upon the earth,
And thither every deed returns,
Which in the generous bosom burns.

There love is warm, and youth is young,
And poetry is yet unsung,
For Virtue still adventures there,
And freely breathes her native air.

And ever, if you hearken well,
You still may hear its vesper bell,
And tread of high-souled men go by,
Their thoughts conversing with the sky.

"Before each van
Prick forth the aery knights, and couch their spears
Till thickest legions close; with feats of arms
From either end of Heaven the welkin burns."

Away! away! away! away!
  Ye have not kept your secret well,
I will abide that other day,
    Those other lands ye tell.

Has time no leisure left for these,
    The acts that ye rehearse?
Is not eternity a lease
    For better deeds than verse?

'Tis sweet to hear of heroes dead,
    To know them still alive,
But sweeter if we earn their bread,
    And in us they survive.

Our life should feed the springs of fame
    With a perennial wave,
As ocean feeds the babbling founts
    Which find in it their grave.

Ye skies drop gently round my breast,
    And be my corselet blue,
Ye earth receive my lance in rest,
    My faithful charger you;

Ye stars my spear-heads in the sky,
　My arrow-tips ye are;
I see the routed foemen fly,
　My bright spears fixed are.

Give me an angel for a foe,
　Fix now the place and time,
And straight to meet him I will go
　Above the starry chime.

And with our clashing bucklers' clang
　The heavenly spheres shall ring,
While bright the northern lights shall hang
　Beside our tourneying.

And if she lose her champion true,
　Tell Heaven not despair,
For I will be her champion new,
　Her fame I will repair.

Low-anchored cloud,
Newfoundland air,
Fountain-head and source of rivers,
Dew-cloth, dream drapery,
And napkin spread by fays;
Drifting meadow of the air,
Where bloom the daisied banks and violets,
And in whose fenny labyrinth
The bittern booms and heron wades;
Spirit of lakes and seas and rivers,
Bear only perfumes and the scent
Of healing herbs to just men's fields!

MAN'S LITTLE ACTS ARE GRAND

Man's little acts are grand,
Beheld from land to land,
There as they lie in time,
Within their native clime.
    Ships with the noontide weigh,
    And glide before its ray
    To some retired bay,
    Their haunt,
    Whence, under tropic sun,
    Again they run,
    Bearing gum Senegal and Tragicant.
For this was ocean meant,
For this the sun was sent,
And moon was lent,
And winds in distant caverns pent.

THE WAVES SLOWLY BEAT

The waves slowly beat,
Just to keep the noon sweet,
And no sound is floated o'er,
Save the mallet on shore,
Which echoing on high
Seems a-calking the sky.

Woof of the sun, ethereal gauze,
Woven of Nature's richest stuffs,
Visible heat, air-water, and dry sea,
Last conquest of the eye;
Toil of the day displayed, sun-dust,
Aerial surf upon the shores of earth,
Ethereal estuary, frith of light,
Breakers of air, billows of heat,
Fine summer spray on inland seas;
Bird of the sun, transparent-winged
Owlet of noon, soft-pinioned,
From heath or stubble rising without song;
Establish thy serenity o'er the fields.

Where gleaming fields of haze
Meet the voyageur's gaze,
And above, the heated air
Seems to make a river there,
The pines stand up with pride
By the Souhegan's side,
And the hemlock and the larch
With their triumphal arch
Are waving o'er its march
 To the sea.
No wind stirs its waves,
But the spirits of the braves
 Hov'ring o'er,
Whose antiquated graves
Its still water laves
 On the shore.
With an Indian's stealthy tread,
It goes sleeping in its bed,
Without joy or grief,
Or the rustle of a leaf,
Without a ripple or a billow,
Or the sigh of a willow,
From the Lyndeboro' hills
To the Merrimack mills.
With a louder din
Did its current begin,

When melted the snow
On the far mountain's brow,
And the drops came together
In that rainy weather.
Experienced river,
Hast thou flowed forever?
Souhegan soundeth old,
But the half is not told,
What names hast thou borne,
In the ages far gone,
When the Xanthus and Meander
Commenced to wander,
Ere the black bear haunted
  Thy red forest-floor,
Or Nature had planted
  The pines by thy shore?

This is my Carnac, whose unmeasured dome
Shelters the measuring art and measurer's home.
Behold these flowers, let us be up with time,
Not dreaming of three thousand years ago,
Erect ourselves and let those columns lie,
Not stoop to raise a foil against the sky.
Where is the spirit of that time but in
This present day, perchance the present line?
Three thousand years ago are not agone,
They are still lingering in this summer morn,
And Memnon's Mother sprightly greets us now,
Wearing her youthful radiance on her brow.
If Carnac's columns still stand on the plain,
To enjoy our opportunities they remain.

TRUE KINDNESS IS A PURE DIVINE AFFINITY

True kindness is a pure divine affinity,
Not founded upon human consanguinity.
It is a spirit, not a blood relation,
Superior to family and station.

Lately, alas, I knew a gentle boy,
   Whose features all were cast in Virtue's mould,
As one she had designed for Beauty's toy,
   But after manned him for her own strong-hold.

On every side he open was as day,
   That you might see no lack of strength within,
For walls and ports do only serve alway
   For a pretence to feebleness and sin.

Say not that Caesar was victorious,
   With toil and strife who stormed the House of Fame,
In other sense this youth was glorious,
   Himself a kingdom wheresoe'er he came.

No strength went out to get him victory,
   When all was income of its own accord;
For where he went none other was to see,
   But all were parcel of their noble lord.

He forayed like the subtile haze of summer,
   That stilly shows fresh landscapes to our eyes,
And revolutions works without a murmur,
   Or rustling of a leaf beneath the skies.

So was I taken unawares by this,
   I quite forgot my homage to confess;
Yet now am forced to know, though hard it is,
   I might have loved him had I loved him less.

Each moment as we nearer drew to each,
  A stern respect withheld us farther yet,
So that we seemed beyond each other's reach,
  And less acquainted than when first we met.

We two were one while we did sympathize,
  So could we not the simplest bargain drive;
And what avails it now that we are wise,
  If absence doth this doubleness contrive?

Eternity may not the chance repeat,
  But I must tread my single way alone,
In sad remembrance that we once did meet,
  And know that bliss irrevocably gone.

The spheres henceforth my elegy shall sing,
  For elegy has other subject none;
Each strain of music in my ears shall ring
  Knell of departure from that other one.

Make haste and celebrate my tragedy;
  With fitting strain resound ye woods and fields;
Sorrow is dearer in such case to me
  Than all the joys other occasion yields.

Is't then too late the damage to repair?
  Distance, forsooth, from my weak grasp hath reft
The empty husk, and clutched the useless tare,
  But in my hands the wheat and kernel left.

If I but love that virtue which he is,
  Though it be scented in the morning air,
Still shall we be truest acquaintances,
  Nor mortals know a sympathy more rare.

The smothered streams of love, which flow
More bright than Phlegethon, more low,
Island us ever, like the sea,
In an Atlantic mystery.
Our fabled shores none ever reach,
No mariner has found our beach,
Scarcely our mirage now is seen,
And neighboring waves with floating green,
Yet still the oldest charts contain
Some dotted outline of our main;
In ancient times midsummer days
Unto the western islands' gaze,
To Teneriffe and the Azores,
Have shown our faint and cloud-like shores.

But sink not yet, ye desolate isles,
Anon your coast with commerce smiles,
And richer freights ye'll furnish far
Than Africa or Malabar.
Be fair, be fertile evermore,
Ye rumored but untrodden shore,
Princes and monarchs will contend
Who first unto your land shall send,
And pawn the jewels of the crown
To call your distant soil their own.

MY LOVE MUST BE
AS FREE

My love must be as free
    As is the eagle's wing,
Hovering o'er land and sea
    And everything.

I must not dim my eye
    In thy saloon,
I must not leave my sky
    And nightly moon.

Be not the fowler's net
    Which stays my flight,
And craftily is set
    T' allure the sight.

But be the favoring gale
    That bears me on,
And still doth fill my sail
    When thou art gone.

I cannot leave my sky
    For thy caprice,
True love would soar as high
    As heaven is.

The eagle would not brook
    Her mate thus won,
Who trained his eye to look
    Beneath the sun.

The Good how can we trust?
Only the Wise are just.
The Good we use,
The Wise we cannot choose.
These there are none above;
The Good they know and love,
But are not known again
By those of lesser ken.
They do not charm us with their eyes,
But they transfix with their advice;
No partial sympathy they feel,
With private woe or private weal,
But with the universe joy and sigh,
Whose knowledge is their sympathy.

NATURE DOTH HAVE HER DAWN EACH DAY

Nature doth have her dawn each day,
    But mine are far between;
Content, I cry, for sooth to say,
    Mine brightest are I ween.

For when my sun doth deign to rise,
    Though it be her noontide,
Her fairest field in shadow lies,
    Nor can my light abide.

Sometimes I bask me in her day,
    Conversing with my mate,
But if we interchange one ray,
    Forthwith her heats abate.

Through his discourse I climb and see,
    As from some eastern hill,
A brighter morrow rise to me
    Than lieth in her skill.

As 'twere two summer days in one,
    Two Sundays come together,
Our rays united make one sun,
    With fairest summer weather.

LET SUCH PURE HATE
STILL UNDERPROP

"Friends, Romans, Countrymen, and Lovers."

Let such pure hate still underprop
Our love, that we may be
Each other's conscience,
And have our sympathy
Mainly from thence.

We'll one another treat like gods,
And all the faith we have
In virtue and in truth, bestow
On either, and suspicion leave
To gods below.

Two solitary stars,—
Unmeasured systems far
Between us roll,
But by our conscious light we are
Determined to one pole.

What need confound the sphere,—
Love can afford to wait,
For it no hour's too late
That witnesseth one duty's end,
Or to another doth beginning lend.

It will subserve no use,
More than the tints of flowers,
Only the independent guest
Frequents its bowers,
Inherits its bequest.

No speech though kind has it,
But kinder silence doles
Unto its mates,
By night consoles,
By day congratulates.

What saith the tongue to tongue?
What heareth ear of ear?
By the decrees of fate
From year to year,
Does it communicate.

Pathless the gulf of feeling yawns,—
No trivial bridge of words,
Or arch of boldest span,
Can leap the moat that girds
The sincere man.

No show of bolts and bars
Can keep the foeman out,
Or 'scape his secret mine
Who entered with the doubt
That drew the line.

No warder at the gate
Can let the friendly in,
But, like the sun, o'er all
He will the castle win,
And shine along the wall.

There's nothing in the world I know
That can escape from love,
For every depth it goes below,
And every height above.
It waits as waits the sky,
Until the clouds go by,
Yet shines serenely on
With an eternal day,
Alike when they are gone,
And when they stay.

Implacable is Love,—
Foes may be bought or teased
From their hostile intent,
But he goes unappeased
Who is on kindness bent.

Packed in my mind lie all the clothes
  Which outward nature wears,
And in its fashion's hourly change
  It all things else repairs.

In vain I look for change abroad,
  And can no difference find,
Till some new ray of peace uncalled
  Illumes my inmost mind.

What is it gilds the trees and clouds,
  And paints the heavens so gay,
But yonder fast-abiding light
  With its unchanging ray?

Lo, when the sun streams through the wood,
  Upon a winter's morn,
Where'er his silent beams intrude
  The murky night is gone.

How could the patient pine have known
  The morning breeze would come,
Or humble flowers anticipate
  The insect's noonday hum,—

Till the new light with morning cheer
　From far streamed through the aisles,
And nimbly told the forest trees
　For many stretching miles?

I've heard within my inmost soul
　Such cheerful morning news,
In the horizon of my mind
　Have seen such orient hues,

As in the twilight of the dawn,
　When the first birds awake,
Are heard within some silent wood,
　Where they the small twigs break,

Or in the eastern skies are seen,
　Before the sun appears,
The harbingers of summer heats
　Which from afar he bears.

My books I'd fain cast off, I cannot read,
'Twixt every page my thoughts go stray at large
Down in the meadow, where is richer feed,
And will not mind to hit their proper targe.

Plutarch was good, and so was Homer too,
Our Shakespeare's life were rich to live again,
What Plutarch read, that was not good nor true,
Nor Shakespeare's books, unless his books were men.

Here while I lie beneath this walnut bough,
What care I for the Greeks or for Troy town,
If juster battles are enacted now
Between the ants upon this hummock's crown?

Bid Homer wait till I the issue learn,
If red or black the gods will favor most,
Or yonder Ajax will the phalanx turn,
Struggling to heave some rock against the host.

Tell Shakespeare to attend some leisure hour,
For now I've business with this drop of dew,
And see you not, the clouds prepare a shower,—
I'll meet him shortly when the sky is blue.

This bed of herd's-grass and wild oats was spread
Last year with nicer skill than monarchs use,
A clover tuft is pillow for my head,
And violets quite overtop my shoes.

And now the cordial clouds have shut all in,
And gently swells the wind to say all's well,
The scattered drops are falling fast and thin,
Some in the pool, some in the flower-bell.

I am well drenched upon my bed of oats;
But see that globe come rolling down its stem,
Now like a lonely planet there it floats,
And now it sinks into my garment's hem.

Drip drip the trees for all the country round,
And richness rare distils from every bough,
The wind alone it is makes every sound,
Shaking down crystals on the leaves below.

For shame the sun will never show himself,
Who could not with his beams e'er melt me so,
My dripping locks,—they would become an elf,
Who in a beaded coat does gayly go.

THE POET'S DELAY

In vain I see the morning rise,
　In vain observe the western blaze,
Who idly look to other skies,
　Expecting life by other ways.

Amidst such boundless wealth without,
　I only still am poor within,
The birds have sung their summer out,
　But still my spring does not begin.

Shall I then wait the autumn wind,
　Compelled to seek a milder day,
And leave no curious nest behind,
　No woods still echoing to my lay?

SALMON BROOK

Salmon Brook,
Penichook,
Ye sweet waters of my brain,
When shall I look,
Or cast the hook,
In your waves again?

Silver eels,
Wooden creels,
These the baits that still allure,
And dragon-fly
That floated by,
May they still endure?

I am the autumnal sun,
With autumn gales my race is run;
When will the hazel put forth its flowers,
Or the grape ripen under my bowers?
When will the harvest or the hunter's moon,
Turn my midnight into mid-noon?
   I am all sere and yellow,
   And to my core mellow.
The mast is dropping within my woods,
The winter is lurking within my moods,
And the rustling of the withered leaf
Is the constant music of my grief.

I am a parcel of vain strivings tied
    By a chance bond together,
  Dangling this way and that, their links
    Were made so loose and wide,
        Methinks,
     For milder weather.

A bunch of violets without their roots,
    And sorrel intermixed,
  Encircled by a wisp of straw
    Once coiled about their shoots,
       The law
    By which I'm fixed.

A nosegay which Time clutched from out
    Those fair Elysian fields,
  With weeds and broken stems, in haste,
    Doth make the rabble rout
       That waste
    The day he yields.

And here I bloom for a short hour unseen,
    Drinking my juices up,
  With no root in the land
    To keep my branches green,
       But stand
    In a bare cup.

Some tender buds were left upon my stem
In mimicry of life,
But ah! the children will not know,
Till time has withered them,
The woe
With which they're rife.

But now I see I was not plucked for naught,
And after in life's vase
Of glass set while I might survive,
But by a kind hand brought
Alive
To a strange place.

That stock thus thinned will soon redeem its hours,
And by another year,
Such as God knows, with freer air,
More fruits and fairer flowers
Will bear,
While I droop here.

ALL THINGS ARE CURRENT FOUND

All things are current found
On earthly ground,
Spirits and elements
Have their descents.

Night and day, year on year,
High and low, far and near,
These are our own aspects,
These are our own regrets.

Ye gods of the shore,
Who abide evermore,
I see your far headland,
Stretching on either hand;

I hear the sweet evening sounds
From your undecaying grounds;
Cheat me no more with time,
Take me to your clime.

WHO SLEEPS BY DAY AND WALKS BY NIGHT

Who sleeps by day and walks by night,
Will meet no spirit but some sprite.

WE SHOULD NOT MIND IF ON OUR EAR THERE FELL

We should not mind if on our ear there fell
Some less of cunning, more of oracle.

THEN SPEND AN AGE IN WHETTING THY DESIRE

Then spend an age in whetting thy desire,
Thou needs't not *hasten* if thou dost *stand fast*.

THEREFORE A TORRENT OF SADNESS DEEP

Therefore a torrent of sadness deep,
Through the strains of thy triumph is heard to sweep.

SUCH NEAR ASPECTS HAD WE

Such near aspects had we
Of our life's scenery.

MY LIFE HAS BEEN THE POEM I WOULD HAVE WRIT

My life has been the poem I would have writ,
But I could not both live and utter it.

WE SEE THE PLANET FALL

We see the *planet* fall,
And that is all.

The other couplets of the *Week* appear as collations in the poems of
which they are a part. For "It doth expand my privacies" and "The
work we choose should be our own" see "Inspiration"; for "Our uninquiring corpses lie more low" see "Travelling"; for "Men are by birth
equal in this, that given" see "Poverty."

Gentle river, gentle river
Swift as glid[e]s thy stream along,
Many a bold Canadian voyageur,
Bravely swelled the gay chanson

Thus of old our valiant fathers,
Many a lagging year agone
Gliding oer the rippling waters,
Taught to banish care in song.

Now the sun's behind the willows,
Now he gleams along the lake,
Hark across the bounding billows
Liquid songs the echoes wake.

Rise Apollo up before us,
E'ne the lark's begun her lay
Let us all in deafning chorus
Praise the glorious king of day.

Thus we lead a life of pleasure,
Thus we while the hours away,
Thus we revel beyond measure,
Gaily live we while we may.

I LOVE A CARELESS STREAMLET

"Long life and success to you."
                              Ubique.

I love a careless streamlet,
That takes a mad-cap leap,
And like a sparkling beamlet
Goes dashing down the steep.

———

Like torrents of the mountain
We've coursed along the lea,
From many a crystal fountain
Toward the far-distant sea.

And now we've gained life's valley,
And through the lowlands roam,
No longer may'st thou dally,
No longer spout and foam.

May pleasant meads await thee,
Where thou may'st freely roll
Towards that bright heavenly sea,
Thy resting place and goal.

And when thou reach'st life's down-hill,
So gentle be thy stream,
As would not turn a grist-mill
Without the aid of steam.

My sincerity doth surpass
  The pretence of optic glass.

Say what are the highlands yonder
Which do keep the spheres asunder
The streams of light which centre in our sun
And those which from some other system run?

Distinguished stranger, system ranger,
Plenipotentiary to our sphere,
Dost thou know of any danger,
War or famine near?

Special envoy, foreign minister,
From the empire of the sky,
Dost thou threaten aught that's sinister
By thy course on high?

Runner of the firmament
On what errand wast thou sent,
Art thou some great general's scout
Come to spy our weakness out?
Sculling thy way without a sail,
Mid the stars and constellations,
The pioneer*er* of a tail
Through the stary nations.
  Thou celestial privateer
We entreat thee come not near.

I think awhile of Love, and while I think,
    Love is to me a world,
    Sole meat and sweetest drink,
    And close connecting link
        Tween heaven and earth.

I only know it is, not how or why,
    My greatest happiness;
    However hard I try,
    Not if I were to die,
        Can I explain.

I fain would ask my friend how it can be,
    But when the time arrives,
    Then Love is more lovely
    Than anything to me,
        And so I'm dumb.

For if the truth were known, Love cannot speak,
    But only thinks and does;
    Though surely out 'twill leak
    Without the help of Greek,
        Or any tongue.

A man may love the truth and practise it,
    Beauty he may admire,
    And goodness not omit,
    As much as may befit
        To reverence.

But only when these three together meet,
        As they always incline,
        And make one soul the seat,
        And favorite retreat
            Of loveliness;

When under kindred shape, like loves and hates
        And a kindred nature,
        Proclaim us to be mates,
        Exposed to equal fates
            Eternally;

And each may other help, and service do,
        Drawing Love's bands more tight,
        Service he ne'er shall rue
        While one and one make two,
            And two are one;

In such case only doth man fully prove
        Fully as man can do,
        What power there is in Love
        His inmost soul to move
            Resistlessly.

———

Two sturdy oaks I mean, which side by side,
        Withstand the winter's storm,
        And spite of wind and tide,
        Grow up the meadow's pride,
            For both are strong

Above they barely touch, but undermined
        Down to their deepest source,
        Admiring you shall find
        Their roots are intertwined
            Insep'rably.

When breathless noon hath paused on hill and vale,
And now no more the woodman plies his axe,
Nor mower whets his scythe,
Somewhat it is, sole sojourner on earth,
To hear the veery on her oaken perch
Ringing her modest trill—
Sole sound of all the din that makes a world,
And I sole ear.
Fondly to nestle me in that sweet melody,
And own a kindred soul, speaking to me
From out the depths of universal being.
O'er birch and hazle, through the sultry air,
Comes that faint sound this way,
On Zephyr borne, straight to my ear.
No longer time or place, nor faintest trace
Of earth, the landscape's shimmer is my only space,
Sole remnant of a world.
Anon that throat has done, and familiar sounds
Swell strangely on the breeze, the low of cattle,
And the novel cries of sturdy swains
That plod the neighboring vale—
And I walk once more confounded a denizen of earth.

THE BLUEBIRDS

In the midst of the poplar that stands by our door,
We planted a bluebird box,
And we hoped before the summer was o'er
A transient pair to coax.

One warm summer's day the bluebirds came
And lighted on our tree,
But at first the wand'rers were not so tame
But they were afraid of me.

They seemed to come from the distant south,
Just over the Walden wood,
And they skimmed it along with open mouth
Close by where the bellows stood.

Warbling they swept round the distant cliff,
And they warbled it over the lea,
And over the blacksmith's shop in a jiff
Did they come warbling to me.

They came and sat on the box's top
Without looking into the hole,
And only from this side to that did they hop,
As 'twere a common well-pole.

Methinks I had never seen them before,
Nor indeed had they seen me,
Till I chanced to stand by our back door,
And they came to the poplar tree.

In course of time they built their nest
And reared a happy brood,
And every morn they piped their best
As they flew away to the wood.

Thus wore the summer hours away
To the bluebirds and to me,
And every hour was a summer's day,
So pleasantly lived we.

They were a world within themselves,
And I a world in me,
Up in the tree—the little elves—
With their callow family.

One morn the wind blowed cold and strong,
And the leaves when whirling away;
The birds prepared for their journey long
That raw and gusty day.

Boreas came blust'ring down from the north,
And ruffled their azure smocks,
So they launched them forth, though somewhat loth,
By way of the old Cliff rocks.

Meanwhile the earth jogged steadily on
In her mantle of purest white,
And anon another spring was born
When winter was vanished quite.

And I wandered forth o'er the steamy earth,
And gazed at the mellow sky,
But never before from the hour of my birth
Had I wandered so thoughtfully.

For never before was the earth so still,
And never so mild was the sky,
The river, the fields, the woods, and the hill,
Seemed to heave an audible sigh.

I felt that the heavens were all around,
And the earth was all below,
As when in the ears there rushes a sound
Which thrills you from top to toe.

I dreamed that I was an waking thought—
A something I hardly knew—
Not a solid piece, nor an empty nought,
But a drop of morning dew.

'Twas the world and I at a game of bo-peep,
As a man would dodge his shadow,
An idea becalmed in eternity's deep—
'Tween Lima and Segraddo.

Anon a faintly warbled note
From out the azure deep,
Into my ears did gently float
As is the approach of sleep.

It thrilled but startled not my soul;
Across my mind strange mem'ries gleamed,
As often distant scenes u[n]roll
When we have lately dreamed

The bluebird had come from the distant South
To his box in the poplar tree,
And he opened wide his slender mouth,
On purpose to sing to me.

MAY MORNING

The school boy loitered on his way to school,
Scorning to live so rare a day by rule.
So mild the air a pleasure 'twas to breathe,
For what seems heaven above was earth beneath.

Soured neighbors chatted by the garden pale,
Nor quarrelled who should drive the needed nail—
The most unsocial made new friends that day,
As when the sun shines husbandmen make hay

How long I slept I know not, but at last
I felt my consciousness returning fast,
For Zephyr rustled past with leafy tread,
And heedlessly with one heel grazed my head.

My eyelids opened on a field of blue,
For close above a nodding violet grew,
A part of heaven it seemed, which one could scent,
Its blue commingling with the firmament.

—True, our converse a stranger is to speech,
Only the practised ear can catch the surging words,
That break and die upon thy pebbled lips.
Thy flow of thought is noiseless as the lapse of thy
own waters,
Wafted as is the morning mist up from thy surface,
So that the passive Soul doth breathe it in,
And is infected with the truth thou wouldst express.

E'en the remotest stars have come in troops
And stooped low to catch the benediction
Of thy countenance. Oft as the day came round,
Impartial has the sun exhibited himself
Before thy narrow skylight—nor has the moon
For cycles failed to roll this way
As oft as elsewhither, and tell thee of the night.
No cloud so rare but hitherward it stalked,
And in thy face looked doubly beautiful.
O! tell me what the winds have writ within these
thousand years,
On the blue vault that spans thy flood—
Or sun transferred and delicately reprinted
For thy own private reading. Somewhat
Within these latter days I've read,
But surely there was much that would have thrilled
the Soul,

Which human eye saw not
I would give much to read that first bright page,
Wet from a virgin press, when Eurus—Boreas—
And the host of airy quill-drivers
First dipped their pens in mist.

Truth–Goodness–Beauty–those celestial thrins,
Continually are born; e'en now the Universe,
With thousand throats—and eke with greener smiles,
Its joy confesses at their recent birth.

In the busy streets, domains of trade,
Man is a surly porter, or a vain and hectoring bully,
Who can claim no nearer kindredship with me
Than brotherhood by law.

I knew a man by sight,
  A blameless wight,
Who, for a year or more,
  Had daily passed my door,
Yet converse none had had with him.

I met him in a lane,
  Him and his cane,
About three miles from home,
  Where I had chanced to roam,
And volumes stared at him, and he at me.

In a more distant place
  I glimpsed his face,
And bowed instinctively;
  Starting he bowed to me,
Bowed simultaneously, and passed along.

Next, in a foreign land
  I grasped his hand,
And had a social chat,
  About this thing and that,
As I had known him well a thousand years.

Late in a wilderness
  I shared his mess,
For he had hardships seen,
  And I a wanderer been;
He was my bosom friend, and I was his.

And as, methinks, shall all,
   Both great and small,
That ever lived on earth,
Early or late their birth,
Stranger and foe, one day each other know.

The loudest sound that burdens here the breeze
Is the wood's whisper; 'tis when we choose to list
Audible sound, and when we list not,
It is calm profound. Tongues were provided
But to vex the ear with superficial thoughts.
When deeper thoughts upswell, the jarring discord
Of harsh speech is hushed, and senses seem
As little as may be to share the extacy.

Anon with gaping fearlessness they quaff
The dewy nectar with a natural thirst,
Or wet their leathern lungs where cranberries lurk,
With sweeter wine than Chian, Lesbian, or Falernian
                                   far.
Theirs was the inward lustre that bespeaks
An open sole—unknowing to exclude
The cheerful day—a worthier glory far
Than that which gilds the outmost rind with darkness
                                  visible—
Virtues that fast abide through lapse of years,
Rather rubbed in than off.

NOON

What time the bittern, solitary bird,
Hides now her head amid the whispering fern,
And not a paddock vexes all the shore—
Nor feather ruffles the incumbent air,
Save where the wagtail interrupts the noon.

I saw the civil sun drying earth's tears—
Her tears of joy that only faster flowed,

Fain would I stretch me by the hig[h]way side,
To thaw and trickle with the melting snow,
That mingled soul and body with the tide,
I too may through the pores of nature flow.

But I alas nor trickle can nor fume,
One jot to forward the great work of Time,
'Tis mine to hearken while these ply the loom,
So shall my silence with their music chime.

LAST NIGHT AS I LAY GAZING
WITH SHUT EYES

Last night as I lay gazing with shut eyes
    Into the golden land of dreams,
I thought I gazed adown a quiet reach
  Of land and water prospect,
    Whose low beach
Was peopled with the now subsiding hum
Of happy industry—whose work is done.

And as I turned me on my pillow o'er,
I heard the lapse of waves upon the shore,
Distinct as it had been at broad noonday,
And I were wandering at Rockaway.

LOVE

We two that planets erst had been
Are now a double star,
And in the heavens may be seen,
Where that we fixed are.

Yet whirled with subtle power along,
Into new space we enter,
And evermore with spheral song
Revolve about one centre.

'Twill soon appear if we but look
At evening into earth's day book,
Which way the great account doth stand
Between the heavens and the land.

When the world grows old by the chimney side,
Then forth to the youngling rocks I glide—
Where over the water, and over the land,
The bells are booming on either hand.

Now up they go ding, then down again dong,
And awhile they swing to the same old song,
And the metal goes round 't a single bound,
A-lulling the fields with i[t]s measured sound—
Till the tired tongue falls with a lengthened boom,
As solemn and loud as the crack of doom.
Then changed is their measure to tone upon tone,
And seldom it is that one sound comes alone,
For they ring out their peals in a mingled throng,
And the breezes waft the loud ding-dong along.

When the echo has reached me in this lone vale,
I am straightway a hero in coat of mail,
I tug at my belt and I march on my post,
And feel myself more than a match for a host.

I am on the alert for some wonderful Thing,
W[h]ich somewhere's a taking place,
'Tis perchance the salute which our planet doth ring
When it meeteth another in space.

—With cunning plates the polished leaves were decked,
Each one a window to the poet's world,
So rich a prospect that you might suspect
In that small space all paradise unfurled.
It was a right delightful road to go,
    marching through pastures of such fair herbage,
O'er hill and dale it lead, and to and fro,
From bard to bard, making an easy stage.

Where ever and anon I slaked my thirst
Like a tired traveller at some poet's well,
Which from the teeming ground did bubbling burst,
And tinkling thence adown the page it fell.
Still through the leaves its music you might hear,
Till other springs fell faintly on the ear.

THE ASSABET

Up this pleasant stream let's row
For the livelong summer's day,
Sprinkling foam where'er we go
In wreaths as white as driven snow—
Ply the oars, away! away!

Now we glide along the shore,
Chucking lillies as we go,
While the yellow-sanded floor
Doggedly resists the oar,
Like some turtle dull and slow.

Now we stem the middle tide
Ploughing through the deepest soil,
Ridges pile on either side,
While we through the furrow glide,
Reaping bubbles for our toil.

Dew before and drought behind,
Onward all doth seem to fly;
Nought contents the eager mind,
Only rapids now are kind,
Forward are the earth and sky.

Sudden music strikes the ear,
Leaking out from yonder bank,
Fit such voyagers to cheer—
Sure there must be naiads here,
Who have kindly played this prank.

There I know the cunning pack
Where yon self-sufficient rill
All its telltale hath kept back,
Through the meadows held its clack,
And now bubbleth its fill.

Silent flows the parent stream,
And if rocks do lie below
Smothers with her waves the din,
As it were a youthful sin,
Just as still and just as slow.

But this gleeful little rill,
Purling round its storied pebble,
Tinkles to the selfsame tune
From December until June,
Nor doth any drought enfeeble.

See the sun behind the willows,
Rising through the golden haze,
How he gleams along the billows—
Their white crests the easy pillows
Of his dew besprinkled rays.

Forward press we to the dawning,
For Aurora leads the way,
Sultry noon and twilight scorning,
In each dew drop of the morning
Lies the promise of a day.

Rivers from the sun do flow,
Springing with the dewy morn,
Voyageurs 'gainst time do row,
Idle noon nor sunset know,
Ever even with the dawn.

Since that first away! away!
Many a lengthy league we've rowed,
Still the sparrow on the spray,
Hastes to usher in the day
With her simple stanza'd ode.

Come let's roam the breezy pastures,
Where the freest zephyrs blow,
Batten on the oak tree's rustle,
And the pleasant insect bustle,
Dripping with the streamlet's flow.

What if I no wings do wear,
Thro' this solid seeming air
I can skim like any swallow
Who so dareth let her follow,
And we'll be a jovial pair.

Like two careless swifts let's sail,
Zephyrus shall think for me—
Over hill and over dale,
Riding on the easy gale,
We will scan the earth and sea.

Yonder see that willow tree
Winnowing the buxom air,
You a gnat and I a bee,
With our merry minstrelsy
We will make a concert there.

One green leaf shall be our screen,
Till the sun doth go to bed,
I the king and you the queen
Of that peaceful little green,
Without any subject's aid.

To our music Time will linger,
And earth open wide her ear,
Nor shall any need to tarry
To immortal verse to marry
Such sweet music as he'll hear.

LOVES FAREWELL

Light hearted, careless, shall I take my way,
When I to thee this being have resigned,
Well knowing where upon a future day,
With usurer's craft, more than myself to find.

EACH MORE MELODIOUS NOTE
I HEAR

Each more melodious note I hear
Brings this reproach to me,
That I alone afford the ear,
Who would the music be.

I WAS BORN UPON THY BANK RIVER

I was born upon thy bank river
My blood flows in thy stream
And thou meanderest forever
  At the bottom of my dream

THE FISHER'S SON

I know the world where land and water meet,
By yonder hill abutting on the main,
One while I hear the waves incessant beat,
Then turning round survey the land again.

Within a humble cot that looks to sea
Daily I breathe this curious warm life,
Beneath a friendly haven's sheltering lea
My noiseless day with myst'ry still is rife.

'Tis here, they say, my simple life began,
And easy credit to the tale I lend,
For well I know 'tis here I am a man,
But who will simply tell me of the end?

These eyes fresh opened spied the far off Sea,
Which like a silent godfather did stand,
Nor uttered one explaining word to me,
But introduced straight godmother Sand.

And yonder still stretches that silent main,
With many glancing ships besprinkled o'er,
And earnest still I gaze and gaze again
Upon the self same waves and friendly shore

Till like a watery humor on the eye
It still appears whichever way I turn,
Its silent waste and mute oerarching sky
With close shut eyes I clearly still discern.

And yet with lingering doubt I haste each morn
To see if Ocean still my gaze will greet,
And with each day once more to life am born,
And tread the earth once more with tott'ring feet.

———

My years are like a stroll upon the beach,
As near the ocean's edge as I can go;
My tardy steps its waves sometimes o'erreach,
Sometimes I stay to let them overflow.

Infinite work my hands find there to do,
Gathering the relics which the waves up cast;
Each tempest scours the deep for something new,
And every time the strangest is the last.

My sole employment 'tis and scrupulous care,
To place my gains beyond the reach of tides,
Each smoother pebble and each shell more rare
Which ocean kindly to my hand confides.

I have but few companions on the shore,
They scorn the strand who sail upon the sea,
Yet oft I think the ocean they've sailed oer
Is deeper known upon the strand to me.

My neighbors sometimes come with lumb'ring carts,
As if they wished my pleasant toil to share,
But straightway go again to distant marts
For only weeds and ballast are their care.

———

'Tis by some strange coincidence if I
Make common cause with ocean when he storms
Who can so well support a separate sky,
And people it with multitude of forms.

Oft in the stillness of the night I hear
Some restless bird presage the coming din,
And distant murmurs faintly strike my ear
From some bold bluff projecting far within.

My stillest depths straightway do inly heave
More genially than rests the summer's calm,
The howling winds through my soul's cordage grieve,
Till every shelf and ledge gives the alarm.

Oft at some ruling star my tide has swelled,
The sea can scarcely brag more wrecks than I,
Ere other influence my waves has quelled
The staunchest bark that floats is high and dry.

I'm guided in the darkest night
By flashes of auroral light,
Which over dart thy eastern home
And teach me not in vain to roam.
Thy steady light on t'other side
Pales the sunset, makes day abide,
And after sunrise stays the dawn,
Forerunner of a brighter morn.

There is no being here to me
But staying here to be
When others laugh I am not glad,
When others cry I am not sad,
But be they grieved or be they merry
I'm supernumerary.
I am a miser without blame
Am conscience stricken without shame.
An idler am I without leisure,
A busy body without pleasure.
I did not think so bright a day
Would issue in so dark a night.
I did not think such sober play
Would leave me in so sad a plight,
And I should be most sorely spent
Where first I was most innocent.
I thought by loving all beside
To prove to you my love was wide,
And by the rites I soared above
To show you my peculiar love.

FRIENDSHIP

Now we are partners in such legal trade,
We'll look to the beginnings, not the ends,
Nor to pay day—knowing true wealth is made
For current stock and not for dividends.

Methinks all things have travelled since you shined,
But only Time, and clouds, Time's team, have moved;
Again foul weather shall not change my mind,
But In the shade I will believe what in the sun I loved.

THEY WHO PREPARE MY EVENING MEAL BELOW

They who prepare my evening meal below
Carelessly hit the kettle as they go
With tongs or shovel,
And ringing round and round,
Out of this hovel
It makes an eastern temple by the sound.

At first I thought a cow-bell right at hand
Mid birches sounded o'er the open land,
Where I plucked flowers
Many years ago,
Spending midsummer hours
With such secure delight they hardly seemed to flow.

My ground is high,
But 'tis not dry,
What you call dew
Comes filtering through;
Though in the sky,
It still is nigh;
Its soil is blue
And virgin too.

IF FROM YOUR PRICE YE
WILL NOT SWERVE

If from your price ye will not swerve,
Why then Ill think the gods reserve
A greater bargain there above,
Out of their sup'rabundant love,
Have meantime better for me cared,
And so will get my stock prepared,
Plows of new pattern, hoes the same,
Designed a different soil to tame,
And sow my seed broadcast in air,
Certain to reap my harvest there.

FRIENDSHIP'S STEADFASTNESS

True friendship is so firm a league
That's maintenance falls into the even tenor
Of our lives, and is no tie,
But the continuance of our lifes thread.

If I would safely keep this new got pelf,
I have no care henceforth but watch myself,
For lo! it goes untended from my sight,
Waxes and wanes secure with the safe star of night.

See with what liberal step it makes its way,
As we could well afford to let it stray
Throughout the universe, with the sun & moon,
Which would dissolve allegiance as soon.

Shall I concern myself for fickleness,
And undertake to make my friends more sure,
When the great gods out of sheer kindliness,
Gave me this office for a sinecure?

DEATH CANNOT COME TOO SOON

Death cannot come too soon
Where it can come at all,
But always is too late
Unless the fates it call.

My life more civil is and free
Than any civil polity.

Ye princes keep your realms
And circumscribed power,
Not wide as are my dreams,
Nor rich as is this hour.

What can ye give which I have not?
What can ye take which I have got?
Can ye defend the dangerless?
Can ye inherit nakedness?

To all true wants time's ear is deaf,
Penurious states lend no relief
Out of their pelf—
But a free soul—thank God—
Can help itself.

Be sure your fate
Doth keep apart its state—
Not linked with any band—
Even the nobles of the land

In tented fields with cloth of gold—
No place doth hold
But is more chivalrous than they are.
And sigheth for a nobler war.
A finer strain its trumpet rings—
A brighter gleam its armor flings.

The life that I aspire to live
No man proposeth me—
No trade upon the street
Wears its emblazonry.

It is a noble country where we dwell,
Fit for a stalwart race to summer in;
From Madawaska to Red River raft,
From Florid keys to the Missouri forks,
See what unwearied (and) copious streams
Come tumbling to the east and southern shore,
To find a man stand on their lowland banks:
Behold the innumerous rivers and the licks
Where he may drink to quench his summer's thirst,
And the broad corn and rice fields yonder, where
His hands may gather for his winter's store.

See the fair reaches of the northern lakes
To cool his summer with their inland breeze,
And the long slumbering Appalachian range
Offering its slopes to his unwearied knees!
See what a long-lipped sea doth clip the shores,
And noble strands where navies may find port;
See Boston, Baltimore, and New York stand
Fair in the sunshine on the eastern sea,
And yonder too the fair green prairie.

See the red race with sullen step retreat,
Emptying its graves, striking the wigwam tent,
And where the rude camps of its brethren stand,
Dotting the distant green, their herds around;
In serried ranks, and with a distant clang,
Their fowl fly o'er, bound to the northern lakes,
Whose plashing waves invite their webbéd feet.

Such the fair reach and prospect of the land,
The journeying summer creeps from south to north
With wearied feet, resting in many a vale;
Its length doth tire the seasons to o'ercome,
Its widening breadth doth make the sea-breeze pause
And spend its breath against the mountain's side:
Still serene Summer paints the southern fields,
While the stern Winter reigns on northern hills.

Look nearer,—know the lineaments of each face,—
Learn the far-travelled race, and find here met
The so long gathering congress of the world!
The Afric race brought here to curse its fate,
Erin to bless,—the patient German too,
Th' industrious Swiss, the fickle, sanguine Gaul,
And manly Saxon, leading all the rest.
All things invite this earth's inhabitants
To rear their lives to an unheard-of height,
And meet the expectation of the land;
To give at length the restless race of man
A pause in the long westering caravan.

The moon now rises to her absolute rule,
And the husbandman and hunter
Acknowledge her for their mistress.
Asters and golden reign in the fields
And the life everlasting withers not.
The fields are reaped and shorn of their pride
But [?] an inward verdure still crowns them
The thistle scatters its down on the pool
And yellow leaves clothe the river—
And nought disturbs the serious life of men.
But behind the sheaves and under the sod
There lurks a ripe fruit which the reapers have not
                                    gathered
The true harvest of the year—the boreal[?] fruit
Which it bears forever.
With fondness annually watering and maturing it.
But man never severs the stalk
Which bears this palatable fruit.

My friends, why should we live?
Life is an idle war a toilsome peace;
   To-day I would not give
One small consent for its securest ease.

   Shall we out-wear the year
In our pavilions on its dusty plain
   And yet no signal hear
To strike our tents and take the road again?

   Or else drag up the slope
The heavy ordnance of nature's train?
   Useless but in the hope,
Some far remote and heavenward hill to gain.

I mark the summer's swift decline
The springing sward its grave clothes weaves
Whose rustling woods the gales confine
The aged year turns on its couch of leaves.

Oh could I catch the sounds remote
Could I but tell to human ear—
The strains which on the breezes float
And sing the requiem of the dying year.

Methinks that by a strict behavior
I could elicit back the brightest star
That lurks behind a cloud.

I HAVE ROLLED NEAR SOME
OTHER SPIRITS PATH

I have rolled near some other spirits path
And with a pleased anxiety have felt
Its purer influence on my opaque mass
But always was I doomed to learn, alas!
I had scarce changed its sidireal time.

How little curious is man
He has not searched his mystery a span
But dreams of mines of treasure
Which he neglects to measure.

For three score years and ten
Walks to and fro amid his fellow men
O'er this small tract of continental land
And never uses a divining wand.

Our uninquiring corpses lie more low
Than our life's curiosity doth go
Our ambitious steps ne'er climb so high
As in their daily sport the sparrows fly

And yonder cloud's borne farther in a day
Than our most vagrant steps may ever stray.
Surely, O Lord, he has not greatly erred,
Who has so little from his threshhold stirred.

He wanders through this low and shallow world
Scarcely his loftier thoughts and hopes unfurled,
Through this low walled world, where his huge sin
Has hardly room to rest and harbor in.

He wanders round until his end draws nigh
And then lays down his aged head to dye
And this is life, this is that famous strife.

ON FIELDS OER WHICH THE REAPER'S
HAND HAS PASS[E]D

On fields oer which the reaper's hand has pass[e]d,
Lit by the harvest moon and autumn sun,
My thoughts like stubble floating in the wind
And of such fineness as October airs,
There after harvest could I glean my life
A richer harvest reaping without toil,
And weaving gorgeous fancies at my will
In subtler webs than finest summer haze.

There is health in thy gray wing
Health of nature's furnishing.
Say thou modern-winged antique,
Was thy mistress ever sick?
In each heaving of thy wing
Thou dost health and leisure bring,
Thou dost waive disease & pain
And resume new life again.

I walk in nature still alone
  And know no one
Discern no lineament nor feature
  Of any creature.

Though all the firmament
  Is oer me bent,
Yet still I miss the grace
  Of an intelligent and kindred face.

I still must seek the friend
Who does with nature blend,
Who is the person in her mask,
He is the man I ask.

Who is the expression of her meaning,
Who is the uprightness of her leaning,
Who is the grown child of her weaning

The center of this world,
The face of nature,
The site of human life,
Some sure foundation
And nucleus of a nation—
At least a private station.

We twain would walk together
Through every weather,
And see this aged nature,
Go with a bending stature.

144

YET LET US THANK THE
PURBLIND RACE

Yet let us Thank the purblind race,
  Who still have thought it good
With lasting stone to mark the place
  Where braver men have stood.

In concord, town of quiet name
  And quiet fame as well,

Ive seen ye, sisters, on the mountain-side
When your green mantles fluttered in the wind
Ive seen your foot-prints on the lakes smooth shore
Lesser than man's, a more ethereal trace,
I have heard of ye as some far-famed race—
Daughters of gods whom I should one day meet—
Or mothers I might say of all our race.
I reverence your natures so like mine
Yet strangely different, like but still unlike
Thou only stranger that hast crossed my path
Accept my hospitality—let me hear
The message which thou bring'st
    Made different from me
  Perchance thou't made to be
  The creature of a different destiny.
I know not who ye are that meekly stand
Thus side by side with man in every land.
When did ye form alliance with our race
Ye children of the moon who in placid nights
Vaulted upon the hills and sought this earth.
Reveal that which I fear ye can not tell
Wherein ye are not I, wherein ye dwell
Where I can never come.
What boots it that I do regard ye so
Does it make suns to shine or crops to grow?
What boots that I never should forget
Thee[?], I have sisters sitting for me yet

And what are sisters
The robust man who can so stoutly strive
In this bleak world is hardly kept alive.
And who is it protects *ye* smooths *your* way

Ye do command me to all virtue ever
And simple truth the law by which we live
Methinks that I can trust your clearer sense
And your immediate knowledge of the truth.
I would obey your influence—one with fate

On shoulders whirled in some eccentric orbit
Just by old Paestum's temples and the perch
Where Time doth plume his wings.

FOG

Dull water spirit—and Protean god
Descended cloud fast anchored to the earth
That drawest too much air for shallow coasts
Thou ocean branch that flowest to the sun
Incense of earth, perfumed with flowers—
Spirit of lakes and rivers, seas and rills
Come to revisit now thy native scenes
Night thoughts of earth—dream drapery
Dew cloth and fairy napkin
Thou wind-blown meadow of the air.

Brother where dost thou dwell?
  What sun shines for thee now?
Dost thou indeed farewell?
  As we wished here below.

What season didst thou find?
  'Twas winter here.
Are not the fates more kind
  Than they appear?

Is thy brow clear again
  As in thy youthful years?
And was that ugly pain
  The summit of thy fears?

Yet thou wast cheery still,
  They could not quench thy fire,
Thou dids't abide their will,
  And then retire.

Where chiefly shall I look
  To feel thy presence near?
Along the neighboring brook
  May I thy voice still hear?

Dost thou still haunt the brink
  Of yonder river's tide?
And may I ever think
  That thou art at my side?

What bird wilt thou employ
 To bring me word of thee?
For it would give them joy,
 'Twould give them liberty,
 To serve their former lord
 With wing and minstrelsy.

A sadder strain has mixed with their song,
 They've slowlier built their nests,
Since thou art gone
 Their lively labor rests.

Where is the finch—the thrush,
 I used to hear?
Ah! they could well abide
 The dying year.

Now they no more return,
 I hear them not;
They have remained to mourn,
 Or else forgot.

Traveller, this is no prison,
He is not dead, but risen.
  Then is there need,
  To fill his grave,
  And truth to save,
  That we should read,—
  In Pursy's favor
  Here lies the engraver.

Here lies the body of this world,
Whose soul alas to hell is hurled.
This golden youth long since was past,
Its silver manhood went as fast,
And iron age drew on at last;
'Tis vain its character to tell,
The several fates which it befell,
What year it died, when 'twill arise,
We only know that here it lies.

By death's favor
Here lies the engraver
And now I think o't
Where lies he not?
If the archangel look but where he lies
He ne'er will get translated to the skies.

A stately music rises on my ear,
Borne on the breeze from some adjacent vale;
A host of knights, my own true ancestors,
Tread to the lofty strains and pass away
In long procession; to this music's sound
The Just move onward in deep serried ranks,
With looks serene of hope, and gleaming brows,
As if they were the temples of the Day.

Gilt by an unseen sun's resplendent ray
They firmly move, sure as the lapse of Time;
Departed worth, leaving these trivial fields
Where sedate valor finds no worthy aim,
And still is Fame the noblest cause of all.

Forward they press and with exalted eye,
As if their road, which seems a level plain,
Did still ascend, and were again subdued
'Neath their proud feet. Forward they move, and leave
The sun and moon and stars alone behind:
And now, by the still fainter strains, I know
They surely pass; and soon their quivering harp,
And faintly clashing cymbal, will have ceased
To feed my ear.

It is the steadiest motion eye hath seen,
A Godlike progress; e'en the hills and rocks
Do forward come, so to congratulate
Their feet; the rivers eddy backward, and
The waves recurl to accompany their march.

Onward they move, like to the life of man,
Which cannot rest, but goes without delay
Right to the gates of Death, not losing time
In its majestic tread to Eternity,
As if Man's blood, a river, flowed right on
Far as the eye could reach, to the Heart of hearts,
Nor eddied round about these complex limbs.

'Tis the slow march of life,—I feel the feet
Of tiny drops go pattering through *my* veins;
Their arteries flow with an Assyrian pace,
And empires rise and fall beneath their stride.

Still, as they move, flees the horizon wall;
The low-roofed sky o'erarches their true path;
For they have caught at last the pace of Heaven,
Their great Commander's true and timely tread.

Lo! how the sky before them is cast up
Into an archèd road, like to the gallery
Of the small mouse that bores the meadow's turf:
Chapels of ease swift open o'er the path,
And domes continuous span the lengthening way.

Tell me ye wise ones if ye can
Whither and whence the race of man.
For I have seen his slender clan
Clinging to hoar hills with their feet
Threading the forest for their meat
Moss and lichens bark & grain
They rake together with might & main
And they digest them with anxiety & pain.
I meet them in their rags and unwashed hair
Instructed to eke out their scanty fare
Brave race—with a yet humbler prayer
Beggars they are aye on the largest scale
They beg their daily bread at heavens door
And if their this years crop alone shou[l]d fail
They neither bread nor begging would know more.
They are the titmans [?] of their race
And hug the vales with mincing pace
Like Troglodites. and fight with cranes.
We walk mid great relations feet
What they let fall alone we eat
We are only able
to catch the fragments from their table
These elder brothers of our race
By us unseen with larger pace
Walk oer our heads, and live our lives
embody our desires and dreams
Anticipate our hoped for gleams

We grub the earth for our food
We know not what is good
Where does the fragrance of our orchards go
Our vineyards while we toil below—
A finer race and finer fed
Feast and revel above our head.
The tints and fragrance of the flowers & fruits
Are but the crumbs from off their table
While we consume the pulp and roots
Some times we do assert our kin
And stand a moment where once they have been
We hear their sounds and see their sights
And we experience their delights—
But for the moment that we stand
Astonished on the Olympian land
We do discern no traveller's face
No elder brother of our race.
To lead us to the monarch's court
And represent our case.
But straightway we must journey back
retracing slow the arduous track,
Without the privilege to tell
Even, the sight we know so well.

The Earth
Which seems so barren once gave birth
To heroes—who oerran her plains,
Who plowed her seas and reaped her grains

THE HERO

What doth he ask?
Some worthy task.
Never to run
Till that be done,
that never done
Under the sun.
Here to begin
All things to win
By his endeavor
Forever and ever—
Happy and well
On this ground to dwell
This soil subdue
Plant and renew.
By might & main
Hea[l]th & strength gain
So to give nerve
To his slenderness
Yet Some mighty pain
He would sustain.
So to preserve
His tenderness.
Not be deceived
Of suffring bereaved
Not lose his life
By living too well
Nor escape strife
In his lonely cell

And so find out Heaven
By not knowing Hell.
Strength like the rock
To withstand any shock—
Yet some Aaron's rod
Some smiting by god
Occasion to gain
To shed human tears
And to entertain
Still divine fears.
Not once for all, forever, blest,
Still to be cheered out of the west
Not from his heart to banish all sighs
Still be encouraged by the sun rise
Forever to love and to love and to love
Within him, around him—beneath him above
To love is to know, is to feel, is to be
At once 'tis his birth & his destiny
For earthly pleasures
Celestial pains
Heavenly losses
For earthly gains.
Must we still eat
The bread we have spurned
Must we rekindle
The faggots we've burned—
Must we go out
By the poor man's gate
Die by degrees
Not by new fate.

Is then[?] no road
This way my friend
Is there no road
Without any end—
When I have slumbered
I have heard sounds
As travellers passing
Over my grounds—
'Twas a sweet music
Wafted them by
I could not tell
If far off or nigh.
Unless I dreamed it
This was of yore—
But I never told it
To mortal before—
Never remembered
But in my dreams
What to me waking
A miracle seems
If you will give of your pulse or your grain
We will rekindle those flames again
Here will we tarry it is without doubt
Till a miracle putteth that fire out.

At midnight's hour I raised my head
The owls were seeking for their bread
The foxes barked impatient still
At their wan[?] fate they bear so ill—
I thought me of eternities delayed
And of commands but half obeyed—
The night wind rustled through the glade
As if a force of men there staid
The word was whispered through the ranks
And every hero seized his lance
The word was whispered through the ranks
    Advance.

I seek the Present Time,
No other clime,
Life in to-day,
Not to sail another way,
To Paris or to Rome,
Or farther still from home.
That man, whoe'er he is,
Lives but a moral death,
Whose life is not coeval
With his breath.
What are deeds done
Away from home?
What the best essay
On the Ruins of Rome?
The dusty highways,
What Scripture says,
This pleasant weather
And all signs together—
The river's meander,
All things, in short,
Forbid me to wander
In deed or in thought.
In cold or in drouth,
seek Not the sunny South,
But make the whole tour
Of the sunny Present Hour.

For here if thou fail,
Where canst thou prevail?
If you love not
Your own land most,
You'll find nothing lovely
Upon a distant coast.
If you love not
The latest sunset,
What is there in pictures
Or old gems set?

If no man should travel
Till he had the means,
There'd be little travelling
For kings or for Queens.
The means, what are they!
They are the wherewithal
Great expenses to pay;—
Life got, and some to spare,
Great works on hand,
And freedom from care.
Plenty of time well spent,
To use,—
Clothes paid for, and no rent
In your shoes;—
Something to eat,
And something to burn,
And, above all, no need to return;—

For they who come back,
,have they not failed,
Wherever they've ridden
Or steamed it, or sailed?
All your grass hayed,—
All your debts paid,—
All your wills made?
Then you might as well have stayed,
For are you not dead,
Only not buried?

The way unto "Today",
The rail road to "Here,"
They never'll grade that way,
Nor shorten it, I fear.
There are plenty of depots
All the world o'er,
But not a single station
At a man's door;
If we would get near
To the secret of things,
We shall not have to hear
When the engine bell rings.

LOVES INVALIDES ARE NOT THOSE
OF COMMON WARS

Loves invalides are not those of common wars
 More than its scars—
They are not disabled for a higher love
 But taught to look above.

With erring men I have small affair
 Though they can do some harm & do not care.
It is a part of them which I can not commend
A part of them that never was my friend.

And once again
When I went a-maying—
& once or twice more I had seen thee before.
For there grow the May flowe[r]
  (*Epigaea repens*)
& the mt cranberry
  & the screech owl *strepens*

Old meeting-house bell
I love thy music well
It peals through the air
Sweetly full & fair
As in the early times
When I listened to its chimes.

Is consigned to the nine.
I to nature consign.
I am but the [word] of myself.
Without inlet it lies
without outlet it flows
From & to the skies
It comes & it goes
I am its source,
& my life is its course
I am its stoney shore
& the gale that passes oer

Among the worst of men that ever lived
However we did seriously attend
A little space we let our thoughts ascend
Experienced our religion & confessed
'Twas good for us to be there—be anywhere
Then to a heap of apples we addressed
& cleared the topmost rider *sine* care
But our Icarian thoughts returned to ground
And we went on to heaven the long way round.

Among the signs of autumn I perceive
The Roman wormwood (called by learned men
Ambrosia elatior, food for gods,—
For to impartial science the humblest weed
Is as immortal once[?] as the proudest flower—)
Sprinkles its yellow dust over my shoes
As I cross the now neglected garden
—We trample under foot the food of gods
& spill their nectar in each drop of dew—
My honest shoes Fast friends that never stray
far from my couch thus powdered countryfied
Bearing many a mile the marks of their adventure
At the post-house disgrace the Gallic gloss
Of those well dressed ones who no morning dew
Nor Roman wormwood ever have been through
Who never walk but are *transported* rather—
For what old crime of theirs I do not gather

Th' ambrosia of the Gods 's a weed on earth
Their nectar is the morning dew which on
'ly our shoes taste—For they are simple folks
'Tis very fit the ambrosia of the gods
Should be a weed on earth. As nectar is
The morning dew with which we wet our shoes
For the gods are simple folks and we should pine
      upon their humble fare

I saw a delicate flower had grown up 2 feet high
Between the horse's paths & the wheel track
Which Dakin's & Maynards wagons had
Passed over many a time
An inch more to right or left had sealed its fate
Or an inch higher. And yet it lived & flourish[e]d
As much as if it had a thousand acres
Of untrodden space around it—and never
Knew the danger it incurred.
It did not borrow trouble nor invite an
Evil fate by apprehending it.
For though the distant market-wagon
Every other day—inevitably rolled
This way—it just as inevitably rolled
In those ruts—And the same
Charioteer who steered the flower
Upward—guided the horse & cart aside from it.
There were other flowers which you would say
Incurred less danger grew more out of the way
Which no cart rattled near, no walker daily passed.
But at length one rambling deviously
For no rut restrained plucked them
And then it appeared that they stood
Directly in his way though he had come
From farther than the market wagon—

To day I climbed a handsome rounded hill
Covered with hickory trees wishing to see
The country from its top—for low hills
show unexpected prospects—I looked
many miles over a woody low-land
Toward Marlborough Framingham & Sudbury
And as I sat amid the hickory trees

I am the little Irish boy
  That lives in the shanty
I am four years old today
  And shall soon be one and twenty
  I shall grow up
  And be a great man
  And shovel all day
  As hard as I can.

  Down in the deep cut
  Where the men lived
  Who made the Rail road.

for supper
  I have some potatoe
  And sometimes some bread
  And then if it's cold
    I go right to bed.

  I lie on some straw
  Under my fathers coat

  My mother does not cry
  And my father does not scold
  For I am a little Irish Boy
  And I'm four years old.

Every day I go to school
Along the Railroad
It was so cold it made me cry
The day that it snowed.

And if my feet ache
I do not mind the cold
For I am a little Irish boy
& I'm four years old.

I do not fear my thoughts will die
For never yet it was so dry
as to scorch the azure of the sky.
It knows no withering & no drought
Though all eyes crop it ne'er gives out
My eyes my flocks are
Mountains my crops are
I do not fear my flocks will stray
For they were made to roam the day
For they can wander with the latest light
Yet be at home at night.

Cans't thou love with thy mind,
  And reason with thy heart?
Cans't thou be kind,
  And from thy darling part?

Cans't thou range earth sea, & air,
And so meet me everywhere?
Through all events I will pursue thee,
Through all persons I will woo thee.

Indeed indeed, I cannot tell,
Though I ponder on it well,
Which were easier to state,
All my love or all my hate.
Surely, surely, thou wilt trust me
When I say thou dost disgust me.
O, I hate thee with a hate
That would fain annihilate;
Yet sometimes against my will,
My dear friend, I love thee still.
It were treason to our love,
And a sin to God above,
One iota to abate
Of a pure impartial hate.

THE VESSEL OF LOVE, THE VESSEL OF STATE

The vessel of love, the vessel of state,
Each is ballasted with hate.
Every Congress that we hold
Means the union is dissolved.

But though the south is still enslaved,
By that oath the Union's saved,
For 'tis our love and not our hate
Interests us in their fate.

When the toads begin to ring,
Then thinner clothing bring
or Off your greatcoat fling

Forever in my dream & in my morning thought
   Eastward a mount ascends—
But when in the sunbeam its hard outline is sought—
   It all dissolves & ends.
The woods that way are gates—the pastures too slop[e] up
   To an unearthly ground—
But when I ask my mates, to take the staff & cup,
   It can no more be found—
Perchanc[e] I have no shoes fit for the lofty soil
   Where my thoughts graze—
No properly spun clues—nor well strained mid day oil
   Or—must I mend my ways?
It is a promised land which I have not yet earned,
   I have not made beginning
With consecrated hand—I have not even learned
   To lay the underpinning.
The mountain sinks by day—as do my lofty thoughts,
   Because I'm not highminded.
If I could think alway above these hills & warts
   I should see it, though blinded.
It is a spiral path within the pilgrim's soul
   Leads to this mountain's brow
Commencing at his hearth he reache[s] to this goal
   He knows not when nor how.

STRANGE THAT SO MANY FICKLE GODS, AS FICKLE AS THE WEATHER

Strange that so many fickle gods, as fickle as the weather,
Throughout Dame Natures provinces should always pull
       together.

THE DEEDS OF KING AND MEANEST HEDGER

The deeds of king and meanest hedger,
Stand side by side in heaven's ledger.

WAIT NOT TILL I INVITE THEE, BUT OBSERVE

Wait not till I invite thee, but observe
I'm glad to see thee when thou com'st.

GREATER IS THE DEPTH OF SADNESS

Greater is the depth of sadness
Than is any height of gladness.

WHERE I HAVE BEEN

Where I have been
There was none seen.

BETTER WAIT

Better wait
Than be too late.

ON A GOOD MAN

Here lies—the world
There rises one.

MAN MAN IS THE DEVIL

Man Man is the Devil
The source of all evil.

YOU MUST NOT ONLY AIM ARIGHT

You must not only aim aright,
But draw the bow with all your might.

THE CHICADEE

The chicadee
Hops near to me.

ANY FOOL CAN MAKE A RULE

Any fool can make a rule
And every fool will mind it.

ALL THINGS DECAY

All things decay
& so must our sleigh

EXPECTATION

No sound from my forge
Has been heard in the gorge,
But as a brittle cup
I've held the hammer up.

For though the caves were rabitted,
    And the well sweeps were slanted,
Each house seemed not inhabited
    But haunted.

The pensive traveller held his way,
    Silent & melancholy,
For every man an ideot was,
    And every house a folly.

My friends, my noble friends, know ye—
That in my waking hours I think of ye
   Ever[?] in godlike band uncompromised & free

NO EARNEST WORK THAT WILL
EXPAND THE FRAME

No earnest work that will expand the frame,
And give a soundness to the muscles to[o]?
How ye do waste your time!
Pray make it wor[th] the while to live,
Or worth the while to die.
Show us great actions piled on high,
Tasking our utmost strength touching the sky,
As if we lived in a mountainous country.
  Hell were not quite so hard to bear
 If one were honored with its hottest place.
And did ye fear ye should spoil Hell
By making it sublime?

The moon hung low o'er Provence vales,
'Twas night upon the sea,
Fair France was woo'd by Afric gales
And paid in minstrelsy.
Along the Rhone then moves a band,
Their banner in the breeze,
Of mail-clad men with iron hand,
And steel on breast and knees.
The herdsman following his droves
Far in the night alone,
Read faintly through the olive groves,—
'Twas Godfrey of Boulogne

The mist still slumbered on the heights
The glaciers lay in shade,
The stars withdrew with faded lights,
The moon went down the glade.
Proud Jura saw the day from far,
And showed it to the plain;
She heard the din of coming war,
But told it not again.
The goatherd seated on the rocks,
Dreaming of battles none
Was wakened by his startled flocks,—
'Twas Godfrey of Boulogne.

Night hung upon the Danube's stream,
  Deep midnight on the vales,
Along the shore no beacons gleam,
  No sound is on the gales.
The Turkish lord has banished care
  The harem sleeps profound,
Save one fair Georgian sitting there
  Upon the Moslem ground.
The lightning flashed a transient gleam,
  A glancing banner shone,
A host swept swiftly down the stream,—
  'Twas Godfrey of Boulogne.

'Twas noon upon Byzantium,
  On street and tower and sea,
On Europe's edge a warlike hum
  Of gathered chivalry.
A troop went boldly through the throng,
  Of Ethiops, Arabs, Huns,
Jews Greeks and Turk, to right their wrong
  Their swords flashed thousand suns.
Their banner cleaved Byzantium's dust,
  And like the sun it shone,
their armor had acquired no rust,—
  'Twas Godfrey of Boulogne.

WHO EQUALLEST THE
COWARD'S HASTE

Who equallest the coward's haste
And still inspires the faintest heart
Whose lofty fame is not disgraced
Though it assume the lowest part

IVE SEARCHED MY FACULTIES AROUND

Ive searched my faculties around
To learn why life to me was lent
I will attend his faintest sound
And then declare to man what God hath meant

Until at length the north winds blow,
And beating high mid ice and snow,
The sturdy goose brings up the rear,
Leaving behind the cold cold year.

I was made erect and lone
And within me is the bone
Still my vision will be clear
Still my life will not be drear
To the center all is near
Where I sit there is my throne
If age choose to sit apart
If age choose give me the start
Take the sap and leave the heart

Spes sibi quisque
Each one his own hope

Wait not till slaves pronounce the word
  To set the captive free,
Be free yourselves, be not deferred,
  And farewell slavery.

Ye are all slaves, ye have your price,
  And gang but cries to gang.
Then rise, the highest of ye rise,
  I hear your fetters clang.

Think not the tyrant sits afar
  In your own breasts ye have
The District of Columbia
  And power to free the Slave.

The warmest heart the north doth breed,
  Is still too cold and far,
The colored man's release must come
  From outcast Africa.

Make haste & set the captive free!—
  Are ye so free that cry?
The lowest depths of slavery
  Leave freedom for a sigh.

What is your whole republic worth?
  Ye hold out vulgar lures,
Why will ye be disparting earth
  When all of heaven is yours?

He's governéd well who rules himself,
  No despot vetoes him,
There's no defaulter steals his pelf,
  Nor revolution grim.

'Tis neither silver rags nor gold
  'S the better currency,
The only specie that will hold
  Is current honesty.

The minister of state hath cares,
  He cannot get release,
Administer his own affairs,
  Nor settle his own peace,

'Tis easier to treat with kings,
  And please our country's foes,
Than treat with conscience of the things
  Which only conscience knows.

There's but the party of the great,
  And party of the mean,
And if there is an Empire State
  'Tis the upright, I ween.

And when the sun puts out his lamp
We'll sleep serene within the camp,
Trusting to his invet'rate skill
Who leads the stars oer yonder hill,
Whose discipline doth never cease
To watch the slumberings of peace,
And from the virtuous hold afar
The melancholy din of war.—
For ye our sentries still outlie,
The earth your pallet and your screen the sky.

From steadfastness I will not swerve
Remembering my sweet reserve.

With all your kindness shown from year to year
Ye do but civil demons still appear,
Still to my mind
Ye are inhuman and unkind,
And bear an untamed aspect to my sight
After the "civil-suited" night
As if ye had lain out
Like to the Indian scout
Who lingers in the purlieus of the towns
With unexplored grace and savage frowns.

THE FRIEND

The great friend
Dwells at the land's end,
There lives he
Next to the Sea.
Fleets come and go,
  Carrying commerce to and fro,
But still sits he on the sand
And maketh firm that headland.
Mariners steer them by his light
Safely in the darkest night,
He holds no visible communion
For his friendship is a union.
Many men dwell far inland,
But he alone sits on the strand,
Whether he ponders men or books
Ever still he seaward looks,
Feels the sea-breeze on his cheek,
At each word the landsmen speak;
From some distant port he hears
Of the ventures of past years
In this the sullen ocean's roar
Of wrecks upon a distant shore;
In every companions eye
A sailing vessel doth descry;
Marine news he ever reads
And the slightest glances heeds.

Near is India to him
Though his native shore is dim,
But the bark which long was due,
Never—never—heaves in view,
Which shall put an end to commerce
And bring back what it took from us,
(Which shall make Siberia free
Of the climes beyond the Sea)
Fetch the Indies in its hold,
All their spices and their gold,
And men sail the sea no more
The sea itself become a shore,
To a broader deeper sea,
A profounder mystery.

Upon the bank at early dawn
  I hear the cocks proclaim the day,
Though the moon shines securely on,
  As if her course they could not stay.

The stars withhold their shining not
Or singly or in scattered crowds,
But seem like Parthian arrows shot
  By yielding Night mid the advancing clouds.

Far in the east their larum rings,
  As if a wakeful host were there,
And now its early clarion sings
  To warn us sluggard knights beware.

One on more distant perch, more clear,
But fainter, brags him still,
But ah, he promises, I fear,
More than her master's household will fulfil.

The sound invades each silent wood,
  Awakes each slumbering bird,
Till every fowl leads forth her brood,
  Which on her nest the tuneful summons heard.

Methinks that Time has reached his prime,
  Eternity is in the flower,
And this the faint, confused chime
  That ushers in the sacred hour.

And has Time got so forward then?
　From what perennial fount of joy,
Dost thou inspire the hearts of men,
　And teach them how the daylight to employ?

From thy abundance pray impart,
　Who dost so freely spill,
Some bravery unto my heart,
　And let me taste of thy perennial rill.

There is such health and length of years
　In the elixir of thy note,
That God himself more young appears,
　From the rare bragging of thy throat.

Between the traveller and the setting sun,
Upon some drifting sand heap of the shore,
A hound stands o'er the carcass of a man.

Must we still eat
The bread we have spurned?
Must we re kindle
The faggots we've burned?

I'M CONTENTED YOU
SHOULD STAY

I'm contented you should stay
  For ever and aye
If you can take yourself away
  Any day.

He knows no change who knows the true,
   And on it keeps his eye,
Who always still the unseen doth view;
   Only the false & the apparent die.

Things change, but change not far
   From what they are not but to what they are,
Or rather 'tis our ignorance that dies;
   Forever lives the knowledge of the wise.

In this roadstead I have ridden
In this covert I have hidden
Friendly thoughts were cliffs to me
And I hid beneath their lea.

This true people took the stranger
And warm hearted housed the ranger
They received their roving guest,
And have fed him with the best

Whatsoe'er the land afforded
To the stranger's wish accorded,
Shook the olive, stripped the vine,
And expressed the strengthening wine.

And at night they did spread o'er him
What by day they spread before him,
That good-will which was repast
Was his covering at last.

The stranger moored him to their pier
Without anxiety or fear;
By day he walked the sloping land,
   By night the gentle heavens he scanned.

When first his bark stood inland
To the coast of this far Finland,
Sweet-watered brooks came tumbling to the shore
The weary mariner to restore.

And still he stayed from day to day
If he their kindness might repay
But more and more
The sullen waves came rolling to the shore.

And still the more the stranger waited
The less his argosy was freighted,
And still the more he stayed
The less his debt was paid.

So He unfurled his mast
To receive the fragrant blast,
And that same refreshing gale
Which had woo'd him to remain
        Again and again—
It was that filled his sail
        'And drove him to the main.

All day the low hung clouds
        Dropt tears into the sea
And the wind amid the shrouds
        Sighed plaintively.

THE FUNERAL BELL

One more is gone
Out of the busy throng
That tread these paths;
The church bell tolls,
Its sad knell rolls
To many hearths.

Flower bells toll not,
Their echoes roll not
Unto my ear;—
There still perchance,
That gentle spirit haunts
A fragrant bier.

Low lies the pall,
Lowly the mourners all
Their passage grope;—
No sable hue
Mars the serene blue
Of heaven's cope.

In distant dell
Faint sounds the funeral bell,
A heavenly chime;
Some poet there
Weaves the light burthened air
Into sweet rhyme.

THE VIRGIN

With her calm, aspiring eyes
She doth tempt the earth to rise,
With humility over all,
She doth tempt the sky to fall.

In her place she still doth stand
A pattern unto the firm land
While revolving spheres come round
To embrace her stable ground.

SPEECH OF A SAXON EALDERMAN

This life, O king, of men on earth,
Compared with that unknown,
Gave to a pleasant fancy birth,
              Close by thy throne.

———

The hall is swept,
The table set,
And anxious guests are there,
With shrinking forms,
For wintry storms
Go howling through the air.

Thy noble Ealderman and Thegnes
A cheerful blaze prepare,
And while without it snows and rains
              Are merry there.

And presently a sparrow comes
And flutters through the hall,
It barely picks the scattered crumbs,
              And that is all.

The while the hall it flies about,
It laughs the cold to scorn,
But soon it goes a window out,
              And summer's gone.

So is it with this life of men,
Thus do our moments fly,
We flutter round the hall, and then
          We pine, and die.

If this new lore can tell us where
We go when summer's gone,
Or how this soul of ours did fare
          Ere we were born,

If it do this, then should we try
To live as may befit,
So I, for one, gladly do cry,
          Welcome be it!

Whether we've far withdrawn
  Or come more near
Equally the outward form
  Doth no more appear.
Not thou by distance lost
No—for regret doth bind
Me faster to thee now
  Than neighborhood confined.
Where thy love followeth me
Is enough society. [?]
Thy indelible mild eye
  Is my sky.
Whether by land or sea
  I wander to and fro,
Oft as I think of thee
  The heavens hang more low
The pure glance of thy eye
Doth purge the summer's sky,
And thy breath so rare
Doth refine the winter's air.
my feet would weary be
Ere they travelled from thee.
I [discover] by thy face
That we are of one race
Flowed in one vein our blood
Ere the sea found its flood
The worm may [be] divided
And each part become a whole,
But the nobler creature man
May not separate a span.

O nature I do not aspire
To be the highest in thy quire,
To be a meteor in the sky
Or comet that may range on high,
Only a zephyr that may blow
Among the reeds by the river low.
Give me thy most privy place
Where to run my airy race.
In some withdrawn unpublic mead
Let me sigh upon a reed,
Or in the [?] woods with leafy din
Whisper the still evening in,
For I had rather be thy child
And pupil in the forest wild
Than be the king of men elsewhere
And most sovereign slave of care
To have one moment of thy dawn
Than share the city's year forlorn.
Some still work give me to do
Only be it near to you.

GUIDO'S AURORA

The God of day rolls his car up the slopes,
Reining his prancing steeds with steady hand,
The moon's pale orb through western shadows gropes,
While morning sheds its light o'er sea and land.

Castles and cities by the sounding main
Resound with all the busy din of life,
The fisherman unfurls his sails again
And the recruited warrior bides the strife.

The early breeze ruffles the poplar leaves,
The curling waves reflect the washed [?] light,
The slumbering sea with the day's impulse heaves,
While o'er the western hills retires the drowsy night.

The sea birds dip their bills in ocean's foam,
Far circling out over the frothy waves—

———

GREECE

When life contracts into a vulgar span
And human nature tires to be a man,
I thank the gods for Greece
That permanent realm of peace,
For as the rising moon far in the night
Checquers the shade with her forerunning light,
So in my darkest hour my senses seem
To catch from her Acropolis a gleam.
Greece who am I that should remember thee?
Thy Marathon and thy Thermopylae
Is my life vulgar my fate mean
Which on such golden memories can lean?

POVERTY

If I am poor it is that I am proud,
If God has made me naked and a boor
He did not think it fit his work to shroud.

The poor man comes from heaven direct to earth
As stars drop down the sky and tropic beams.
The rich receives in our gross air his birth,
As from low suns are slanted golden gleams.

Men are by birth equal in this that given
Themselves and their condition they are even.
The less of inward essence is to leaven
The more of outward circumstance is given.

Yon sun is naked bare of satellite
Unless our earths and moons that office hold,
Though his perpetual day feareth no night
And his perennial summer dreads no cold.

Where are his gilded rays but in our sky?
His solid disk doth float far from us still,
The orb which through the central way doth fly
Shall naked seem [?] though proudly circumstanced.

Ill leave my mineral wealth hoarded in earth?
Buried in seas in mines and ocean caves
More safely kept than is the merchant's worth,
Which every storm committeth to the waves.

Man kind may delve but cannot my wealth spend,
If I no partial store appropriate
no armed ships into the Indies send
To rob me of my orient estate

The rich man's clothes keep out the genial sun
But scarce defend him from the piercing cold
If he did not his heavenly garment shun
He would not need to hide beneath a fold.

I'M NOT ALONE

I'm not alone
If I stand by myself,
But more than one,
And not [?] in my own pelf.

I'm understood
If my intent is good,
For who obeys
The truth finds his own praise.

What sought th[e]y th[u]s afar
They sought a faith's pure shrine.

Seek! shall I seek! The Gods above should give,
They have enough & w[e] do poorly live.

"I ask today for no external thing
For sight of upland hill and waving tree,
I do not wish to see the glancing wing
Of bird nor hear with trembling heart her melody,
I ask for that which is our whole life's light,
for the perpetual, true, & clear insight."

Away! away! Thou speakest to me of things
which in all my endless life I have found
not and shall not find.
                                    [Word] to Music
Thy lot, or portion of life, is seeking after
thee; therefore be at rest from seeking
after it. [Word?]

MUSIC

Far from this atmosphere that music sounds
Bursting some azure chink in the dull clouds
Of sense that overarch my recent years
And steal his freshness from the noonday sun.
Ah, I have wandered many ways and lost
The boyant step, the whole responsive life
That stood with joy to hear what seemed then
Its echo, its own harmony borne back
Upon its ear. This tells of better space,
Far far beyond the hills the woods the clouds
That bound my low and plodding valley life,
Far from my sin, remote from my distrust,
When first my healthy morning life perchance
Trod lightly as on clouds, and not as yet
My weary and faint hearted noon had sunk
Upon the clod while the bright day went by.
    Lately, I feared my life was empty, now
I know though a frail tenement that it still
Is worth repair, if yet its hollowness
Doth entertain so fine a guest within, and through
Its empty aisles there still doth ring
Though but the echo of so high a strain;
It shall be swept again and cleansed from sin
To be a thoroughfare for celestial airs;
Perchance the God who is proprietor
Will pity take on his poor tenant here
And countenance his efforts to improve
His property and make it worthy to revert,
At some late day Unto himself again.

I'm thankful that my life doth not deceive
Itself with a low loftiness, half height,
And think it soars when still it dip its way
Beneath the clouds on noiseless pinion
Like the crow or owl, but it doth know
The full extent of all its trivialness,
Compared with the splendid heights above.
    See how it waits to watch the mail come in
While 'hind its back *the sun goes out perchance.*
And yet their lumbering cart brings me no word
Not one scrawled leaf such as my neighbors get
To cheer them with the slight events forsooth
Faint ups and downs of their far distant friends—
And now tis passed. What next? See the long train
Of teams wreathed in dust, their atmosphere;
Shall I attend until the last is passed?
Else why these ears that hear the leader's bells
Or eyes that link me in procession.
But hark! the drowsy day has done its task,
Far in yon hazy field where stands a barn
Unanxious hens improve the sultry hour
And with contented voice now brag their deed—
A new laid egg—Now let the day decline—
Th[e]y'll lay another by tomorrow's sun.

MANHOOD

I love to see the man, a long-lived child,
As yet uninjured by all worldly taint
As the fresh infant whose whole life is play.
'Tis a serene spectacle for a serene day;
But better still I love to contemplate
The mature soul of lesser innocence,
Who hath travelled far on life's dusty road
Far from the starting point of infancy
And proudly bears his small degen'racy
Blazon'd on his memorial standard high
Who from the sad experience of his fate
Since his bark struck on that unlucky rock
Has proudly steered his life with his own hands.
Though his face harbors less of innocence
Yet there do chiefly lurk within its depths
Furrowed by care, but yet all over spread
With the ripe bloom of a self-wrought content
Noble resolves which do reprove the gods
And it doth more assert man's eminence
Above the happy level of the brute
And more doth advertise me of the heights
To which no natural path doth ever lead
No natural light can ever light our steps,
—But the far-piercing ray that shines
From the recesses of a brave man's eye.

The moon moves up her smooth and sheeny path
Without impediment; and happily
The brook Glides by lulled by its tinkling;
Meteeors drop down the sky without chagrin
And rise again; but my cares never rest.
No charitable laws alas cut me
An easy orbit round the sun, but I
Must make my way through rocks and seas and earth
my steep and devious way Uncertain still.
My current never rounds into a lake
In whose fair heart the heavens come to bathe
Nor does my life drop freely but a rod[?]
By its resistless course
As Meteors do.

LIFE

My life is like a stately warrior horse,
That walks with fluent pace along the way,
And I the upright horseman that bestrides
His flexuous back, feeding my private thoughts.—
Alas, when will this rambling head and neck
Be welded to that firm and brawny breast?—
But still my steady steed goes proudly forth,
Mincing his stately steps along the road;
The sun may set, the silver moon may rise,
But my unresting steed holds on his way.
He is far gone ere this, you fain would say,
He is far going. Plants grow and rivers run;
You ne'er may look upon the ocean waves,
At morn or eventide, but you will see
Far in th' horizon with expanded sail,
Some solitary bark stand out to sea,
Far bound—well so my life sails far,
To double some far cape not yet explored.
A cloud ne'er standeth in the summer's sky,
The eagle sailing high, with outspread wings
Cleaving the silent air, resteth him not
A moment in his flight, the air is not his perch.
Nor doth my life fold its unwearied wings,
And hide its head within its downy breast,
But still it plows the shoreless seas of time,
Breasting the waves with an unsanded bow.

PRAY TO WHAT EARTH DOES THIS
SWEET COLD BELONG

Pray to what earth does this sweet cold belong,
Which asks no duties and no conscience?
The moon goes up by leaps her cheerful path
In some far summer stratum of the sky,
While stars with their cold shine bedot her way.
The fields gleam mildly back upon the sky,
And far and near upon the leafless shrubs
The snow dust still emits a silvery light.
Under the hedge, where drift banks are their screen,
The titmice now pursue their downy dreams,
As often in the sweltering summer nights
The bee doth drop asleep in the flower cup,
When evening overtakes him with his load.
By the brooksides, in the still genial night,
The more adventurous wanderer may hear
The crystals shoot and form, and winter slow
Increase his rule by gentlest summer means.

When the oaks are in the gray
Then Farmers plant away.

Whate'er we leave to God, God does,
   And blesses us;
The work we choose should be our own,
   God lets alone.

If with light head erect I sing,
   Though all the muses lend their force,
From my poor love of anything,
   The verse is weak and shallow as its source.

But if with bended neck I grope,
   Listening behind me for my wit,
With faith superior to hope,
   More anxious to keep back than forward it,

Making my soul accomplice there
   Unto the flame my heart hath lit,
Then will the verse forever wear,—
   Time cannot bend the line which God hath writ.

Always the general show of things
   Floats in review before my mind,
And such true love and reverence brings,
   That sometimes I forget that I am blind.

But now there comes unsought, unseen,
   Some clear, divine electuary,
And I who had but sensual been,
   Grow sensible, and as God is, am wary.

I hearing get who had but ears,
    And sight, who had but eyes before,
I moments live who lived but years,
    And truth discern who knew but learning's lore.

I hear beyond the range of sound,
    I see beyond the range of sight,
New earths and skies and seas around,
    And in my day the sun doth pale his light.

A clear and ancient harmony
    Pierces my soul through all its din,
As through its utmost melody,—
    Farther behind than they—farther within.

More swift its bolt than lightning is,
    Its voice than thunder is more loud,
It doth expand my privacies
    To all, and leave me single in the crowd.

It speaks with such authority,
    With so serene and lofty tone,
That idle Time runs gadding by,
    And leaves me with Eternity alone.

Then chiefly is my natal hour,
    And only then my prime of life,
Of manhood's strength it is the flower,
    'Tis peace's end and war's beginning strife.

'T 'hath come in summer's broadest noon,
　By a grey wall or some chance place,
Unseasoned time, insulted June,
　And vexed the day with its presuming face.

Such fragrance round my couch it makes,
　More rich than are Arabian drugs,
That my soul scents its life and wakes
　The body up beneath its perfumed rugs.

Such is the Muse—the heavenly maid,
　The star that guides our mortal course,
Which shows where life's true kernel's laid,
　Its wheat's fine flower, and its undying force.

She with one breath attunes the spheres,
　And also my poor human heart,
With one impulse propels the years
　Around, and gives my throbbing pulse its start.

I will not doubt forever more,
　Nor falter from a steadfast faith,
For though the system be turned o'er,
　God takes not back the word which once he saith.

I will then trust the love untold
　Which not my worth nor want has bought,
Which wooed me young and woos me old,
　And to this evening hath me brought.

My memory I'll educate
   To know the one historic truth,
Remembering to the latest date
   The only true and sole immortal youth.

Be but thy inspiration given,
   No matter through what danger sought,
I'll fathom hell or climb to heaven,
   And yet esteem that cheap which love has bought.

––––––

     Fame cannot tempt the bard
       Who's famous with his God,
     Nor laurel him reward
       Who hath his Maker's nod.

INSPIRATION

If thou wilt but stand by my ear,
When through the field thy anthem's rung,
When that is done I will not fear
But the same power will abet my tongue.

DELAY

No generous action can delay
Or thwart our higher, steadier aims,
But if sincere and true are they,
It will arouse our sight and nerve our frames.

Thank God who seasons thus the year,
    And sometimes kindly slants his rays;
For in his winter he's most near
    And plainest seen upon the shortest days.

Who gently tempers now his heats,
    And then his harsher cold, lest we
Should surfeit on the summer's sweets,
    Or pine upon the winter's crudity.

A sober mind will walk alone,
    Apart from nature, if need be,
And only its own seasons own;
    For nature leaving its humanity.

Sometimes a late autumnal thought
    Has crossed my mind in green July,
And to its early freshness brought
    Late ripened fruits, and an autumnal sky.

. . . .

The evening of the year draws on,
    The fields a later aspect wear;
Since Summer's garishness is gone,
    Some grains of night tincture the noontide air.

Behold! the shadows of the trees
   Now circle wider 'bout their stem,
Like sentries that by slow degrees
   Perform their rounds, gently protecting them.

And as the year doth decline,
   The sun allows a scantier light;
Behind each needle of the pine
   There lurks a small auxiliar to the night.

I hear the cricket's slumbrous lay
   Around, beneath me, and on high;
It rocks the night, it soothes the day,
   And everywhere is Nature's lullaby.

But most he chirps beneath the sod,
   When he has made his winter bed;
His creak grown fainter but more broad,
   A film of autumn o'er the summer spread.

Small birds, in fleets migrating by,
   Now beat across some meadow's bay,
And as they tack and veer on high,
   With faint and hurried click beguile the way.

Far in the woods, these golden days,
   Some leaf obeys its Maker's call;
And through their hollow aisles it plays
   With delicate touch the prelude of the Fall.

Gently withdrawing from its stem,
    It lightly lays itself along
Where the same hand hath pillowed them,
    Resigned to sleep upon the old year's throng.

The loneliest birch is brown and sere,
    The furthest pool is strewn with leaves,
Which float upon their watery bier,
    Where is no eye that sees, no heart that grieves.

The jay screams through the chestnut wood;
    The crisped and yellow leaves around
Are hue and texture of my mood—
    And these rough burrs my heirlooms on the ground.

The threadbare trees, so poor and thin—
    They are no wealthier than I;
But with as brave a core within
    They rear their boughs to the October sky.

Poor knights they are which bravely wait
    The charge of Winter's cavalry,
Keeping a simple Roman state,
    Discumbered of their Persian luxury.

The willows droop,
The alders stoop,
The pheasants group
   Beneath the snow;
The fishes glide
From side to side,
In the clear tide,
   The ice below.

The ferret weeps,
The marmot sleeps,
The owlet keeps
   In his snug nook.
The rabbit leaps,
The mouse out-creeps,
The flag out-peeps,
   Beside the brook.

The snow-dust falls,
The otter crawls,
The partridge calls
   Far in the wood;
The traveller dreams,
The tree-ice gleams,
The blue jay screams
   In angry mood.

The apples thaw,
The ravens caw,
The squirrels gnaw
   The frozen fruit;
To their retreat
I track the feet
Of mice that eat
   The apple's root.

The axe resounds,
And bay of hounds,
And tinkling sounds
   Of wintry fame;
The hunter's horn
Awakes the dawn
On field forlorn,
   And frights the game.

The tinkling air
Doth echo bear
To rabbit's lair,
   With dreadful din;
She scents the air,
And far doth fare,
Returning where
   She did begin.

The fox stands still
'Upon the hill
Not fearing ill
   From trackless wind.
But to his foes
The still wind shows
In treacherous snows
   His tracks behind.

Now melts the snow
In the warm sun.
The meadows flow,
The streamlets run.
The spring is born,
The wild bees bum,
The insects hum,
And trees drop gum.
And winter's gone,
And summer's come.

The chic-a-dee
Lisps in the tree,
The winter bee
   Not fearing frost;
The small nuthatch
The bark doth scratch
Some worm to catch
   At any cost.

The catkins green
Cast o'er the scene
A summer sheen,
A genial glow.

I melt, I flow,
    And rippling run,
Like melting snow
    In this warm sun.

WHY DO THE SEASONS CHANGE?
AND WHY

Why do the seasons change? and why
Does Winter's stormy brow appear?
Is it the word of him on high,
Who rules the changing varied year.

FRIENDS! THAT PARTING TEAR RESERVE IT

Friends! that parting tear reserve it,
Tho' 'tis doubly dear to me!
Could I think I did deserve it,
How much happier would I be.

IN ADAMS FALL

In Adams fall
We sinned all.
In the new Adam's rise
We shall all reach the skies.

IN TIMES OF YORE, 'TIS SAID,
THE SWIMMING ALDER

In times of yore, 'tis said, the swimming Alder,
Fashioned rude, with branches lopt, and stript
Of its smooth coat,—
Where fallen tree was not, and rippling stream's
Vast breadth forbade adventurous leap,
The brawny swain did bear secure to farthest shore.

The Book has passed away,
And with the book the lay,
Which in my youthful days I loved to ponder;
Of curious things it told,
How wise Men Three of old,   (Gotham)
In bowl did venture out to sea,—
And darkly hints their future fate.

If men have dared the Main to tempt
In such frail bark, why may not washtub round,
Or bread-trough square? oblong?—suffice to cross
The purling wave? and gain the destined port.

BY HIS GOOD GENIUS PROMPTED
OR THE POWER

By his good genius prompted or the power
That fills the mind with

INDEX OF TITLES AND FIRST LINES

Titles are given in roman; lifted first lines when used as titles are italicized and set within quotation marks; first lines are given in quotation marks.*

---

* Since the titles (Thoreau's or otherwise) of variant versions are also listed in this index, each variant title is ascribed to the first page of its related basic text. Thus, the title "Winter Memories" was given, in *Poems of Nature,* to one version of "Within the circuit of this plodding life"; and a reader looking for the poem "Winter Memories" and referred here to p. 3 will find on that page Thoreau's final version of the poem in the form of "Within the circuit of this plodding life"—even though he will not find the title "Winter Memories" there. (In the Critical Edition, however, all titled and untitled variant versions are recorded in the textual notes.)

249

250

251

252

Date Due

MAY 4 1965

NOV 2 7 1972